Alexius Meinong's
Elements of Ethics

OTHER PUBLICATIONS BY M.L. SCHUBERT KALSI

Meinong's Theory of Knowledge, *Martinus Nijhoff,* The Hague, 1987.* (Reviewed in **M.M. Hurley and Staff, Summary and Comments)**

Alexius Meinong On Objects of Higher Order and Husserl's Phenomenology, *Martinus Nijhoff,* The Hague, 1978.* (Reviewed in **Philosophy and Phenomenological Research** and **Choice.**)

Alexius Meinong, On Emotional Presentation, Translation with an Introduction. Northwestern University Press, Evanston, Ill., 1972. (Reviewed in **Choice** and frequently referenced.)

*NOTE
All Martinus Nijhoff publications are available from Kluwer Academic Publishers.

Alexius Meinong's Elements of Ethics

with Translation of the Fragment *Ethische Bausteine*

by

Marie-Luise Schubert Kalsi

Southwest Texas State University

KLUWER ACADEMIC PUBLISHERS

DORDRECHT / BOSTON / LONDON

Library of Congress Cataloging-in-Publication Data

```
Schubert Kalsi, Marie-Luise.
   Alexius Meinong's Elements of ethics : with translation of the
fragment Ethische Bausteine / by Marie-Luise Schubert Kalsi.
      p.   cm.
   Includes bibliographical references and index.
   ISBN 0-7923-3803-0 (alk. paper)
   1. Meinong, A. (Alexius), 1853-1920. 2. Ethics.   I. Meinong, A.
(Alexius), 1853-1920.  Ethische Bausteine. English. II. Title.
B3309.M24S354  1996
   170'.92--dc20
                                                      95-40136
```

ISBN 0-7923-3803-0

Published by Kluwer Academic Publishers,
P.O. Box 17, 3300 AA Dordrecht, The Netherlands.

Kluwer Academic Publishers incorporates
the publishing programmes of
D. Reidel, Martinus Nijhoff, Dr W. Junk and MTP Press.

Sold and distributed in the U.S.A. and Canada
by Kluwer Academic Publishers,
101 Philip Drive, Norwell, MA 02061, U.S.A.

In all other countries, sold and distributed
by Kluwer Academic Publishers Group,
P.O. Box 322, 3300 AH Dordrecht, The Netherlands.

I thank Barbara Benson for preparing
the camera ready copy

Printed on acid-free paper

TABLE OF CONTENTS

Preface

by

Roderick M. Chisholm

The present book is a translation of and commentary on Meinong's **Ethische Bausteine**, his most important work on moral philosophy.

Hofrat Dr. Rudolf Kindinger tells us in his Introduction to Band III of the **Gesamtausgabe** that the manuscript had been edited by Ernst Mally in 1921, two years after Meinong's death. Two pages of the manuscript were missing, but fortunately the loss does not affect the general sense of the work.

Professor Schubert Kalsi, who has previously given us translations of Meinong's treatise **On Emotional Presentation**[1] and Meinong's **Objects of Higher Order and Husserl's Phenomenology**[2], now provides us with a welcome addition to Meinong studies. Her book is a significant contribution to Meinong studies as well as to ethics and to the origins of deontic logic.

---

[1] **Alexius Meinong: On Emotional Presentation**, Translation and Introduction, Northwestern University Press, Evanston, IL, 1972.
[2] **Alexius Meinong on Objects of Higher Order and Husserl's Phenomenology**, Martinus Nijhoff, Den Haag, 1978.

Introduction

Meinong poses an immense challenge to his interpreters. He did not develop a system. He tackled many problems, he developed intriguing and innovative ideas, and, over the long years of his productive life, he changed his basic philosophic attitude in profound ways. His texts are often obscure, and the interpreter is faced with the task of bringing order into Meinong's thought and with constructing a cohesive system from his ever-changing and diffusive analysis of ideas.

This book is an account of some important aspects of Meinong's philosophy in the context of modern discussions in value theory and ontology. It contains three sections: 1) my critical exposition of Meinong's simplified ontology, theory of presentation of objects, his theory of objects, *Gegenstandstheorie*, and his theory of the apriori. This is followed by a discussion of concepts in general, precision concepts and precision objects in particular in connection with the law of contradiction, and then the unavoidable analysis of the infelicitous so-called "incomplete objects," also called "incompletely determined object," which have given much distress to contemporary philosophers concerning themselves with Meinong and Austrian philosophy[3]. 2) my interpretation of Meinong's general theory of values, especially his attempt at the development of a deontic logic; and 3) my translation into English of Meinong's posthumously published monograph ***Ethische Bausteine*** (**Elements of Ethics, 1923**) together with Meinong's own appended notes.

Meinong's theory of values is based on the theory of objects and the theory of the apriori, proceeding from empirical data and empirical generalizations. This book is a continuation of my previous work on Meinong[4]. There, I initiated my study of Meinong's theories of values

---

[3] See the bibliography of this book.
[4] **On Emotional Presentation; Meinong on Objects of Higher Order...; Meinong's Theory of Knowledge**.

and of objects of higher order as well as his epistemology of perception, memory, time, and evidence.

Meinong's theory of objects has influenced various systems of modern logic. His "universe" is used in the writings of many authors[5]. My claim is that his ontology has been, in many cases, misunderstood in the English-speaking countries because the primary sources, mostly not translated, are inaccessible in their complicated and, unfortunately, often confusing style; and some philosophers using Meinong's so-called ontology have had to rely on outdated or incorrect sources[6]. My interpretation of the mature Meinong's theory of objects and apriori knowledge ought to be generally acceptable. I see it as a correct, although simplified, account of the "Meinongian universe" which will be useful for any logician and value theorist. When I speak of "the mature Meinong," I refer to the Meinong of **Über die Stellung der Gegenstandstheorie im System der Wissenschaften,** who was keenly aware of the new developments in logic and mathematics, especially in geometry, and who saw clearly the implication these theories had for epistemology and ontology and, consequently, for value theory and ethics. (The very late Meinong turns again to extremely complicated and inconsistent ontological speculations which are very interesting in themselves but not of much help for one looking for clarity and simplicity[7].)

In Section 1 of this book, Meinong's Theory of Objects is discussed. It has become important in modern logic, especially for those systems striving for an ontologically neutral logic and also for deontic logic[8]. The Theory of Objects is not at all concerned with questions of existence or nonexistence. It includes logical, mathematical, and semantic problems. It concerns itself with any object of thought – existing or not, possible, necessary, even impossible – with its properties and relationships to other objects. Any nonempirical, i.e., apriori, consideration of any object, regardless of its ontological status, falls into the Theory of Objects.

---

[5] e.g., Chisholm, Haller, Putnam, Routley, Parsons, Lambert, Rappaport.
[6] Fortunately Über Annahmen II has appeared in English.
[7] See especially the lecture notes in Ergänzungsband.
[8] Some of the contemporary writers to be mentioned are Richard Routley, Karel Lambert, Hilary Putnam, W. V. Quine, J. Hintikka, von Wright.

In this book, I concentrate on the apriori, which plays a prominent part in Meinong's late theory of values and valuations and which is the mode of cognition in his Theory of Objects[9]. As the question of apriori has become important again in recent times, a new study of Meinong's theory of the apriori is most timely and important. Apriori knowledge is not only of logical truths and truths by definition, but any judgments which are not judgments of existence or judgments dependent on judgments of existence are apriori judgments. "Existence," roughly speaking, refers to spatio-temporal occurrences of individual objects and perceptual properties and relations.

For Meinong, all judgments and statements are apriori which are of objects that do not exist or whose existence is not of any import at the moment. Apriori judgments are of non-existing relationships, i.e., those that are not externally perceived but only thought between objects that themselves may or may not exist, as for example the relation of similarity between two apples which I ate yesterday or between two creatures of my fantasy. Also judgments of non-perceptible properties of existing or nonexisting objects are apriori as well as are judgments of abstract objects like numbers and geometric objects. Examples include nation, melody, inheritance, superior, beautiful, loyal. The apriori can proceed from and be based on empirical knowledge; it can also be purely apriori. Mathematical theorems are purely apriori; judging the beauty of an object or the being of a nation is apriori, but based on empirical knowledge of the object which is judged to be beautiful or to be a nation.

The extent of the apriori and its relevance and acceptability from present day's philosophical standpoint is put into focus. The result of the discussions is also important for questions concerning values: there can be apriori value judgments only if there is apriori knowledge at all.

In the second section of this book Meinong's general theory of values and valuations are studied. Meinong began writing on a general theory of values in 1884 (**Psychologisch-ethische Untersuchungen zur**

---

[9] The term "valuations" can be understood in two ways: 1) it is the attribution of a negative of positive value to an object, and 2) it is the presentation of a value alone by a feeling. Attribution and feeling occur in the subject of the valuation. The value subject, on the other hand, is the person for whom the object has value. The subject of the valuation and of the value does not have to be the same.

allgemeinen Werttheorie) proceeding empirically from the basis of the value theory of national economics (**Nationalökonomie**), also using partially its technical vocabulary which, however, is not relevant anymore for our understanding of his theories. It is an interesting side note that he took economics as an example to follow, just as some modern moral philosophers take the example of evolving attitudes and procedures in legal theories as examples for their own work[10]. The reader will notice the economics background in the appended translation.

The empirical descriptive approach did not lead to satisfactory results. During the decade following the first of his books on ethics, Meinong developed a new ontology which is quite complicated and many faceted. I leave that ontology behind me now, and will only mention that it leads to the Theory of Objects through a theoretical analysis of the psychic presentations of having ideas of individual objects, properties, relations, etc., of making judgments (the psychological counterpart of statements). Meinong then turned to a theoretical analysis of the psychic presentation of values, valuations, and obligations and, from these, arrived at a theory of absolute values (also a part of the Theory of Objects) in **On Emotional Presentation** where he not only believed that value statements were apriori but also that values subsisted, that is, their being was existence-free[11]. The ontological status of values themselves remains undeclared in the attached translation, but the apriori character of certain value judgments remains untouched. Meinong turned back to a more empirical analysis of valuations and the laws by which the relationships between them could be generally described. However. this study served as the basis of a general theory of absolute values which is apriori. This is the beginning of deontic logic.

Meinong wanted to show that ethics is a special case of a general value theory, and that value theory is based on the psychological analysis of value experiences. The experiences of the ego as directed to or concerning an alter are analyzed without specific considerations of who the ego and the alter are. This was a new approach in value theory. Here a value

---

[10]   For example Vincent Luizzi, **A Case for Legal Ethics**, State University of New York Press, 1993.

[11]   The vocabulary of **On Emotional Presentation** is strikingly different from the vocabulary of his other writings in ethics.

line is introduced. This innovation appears in several of the above-mentioned writings and is analyzed in Section 2, Chapter Seven. This analysis leads to the classes of what ought to be done or what ought not to be done and what is permissible to do and what is not permissible to do, and what is indifferent in respect to obligation and permission. In early writings the approach was intended to be empirical as "methodical questioning of moral common sense."

After 1910 the inquiries take on a different character. In the meantime Meinong has developed his "Theory of Objects" which amounts to a purely apriori analysis of the characteristics of objects. It is discussed in detail in Section 1, chapters One, Two, and Three. Value concepts as they are pregiven in ordinary use are theoretically analyzed and so are the relations between them. It is not the valuation which makes the value. There are values given with objects which have them, and there are mistakes in valuations. Of course, values are found by asking what is valued. This is not circular. The beginning is always empirical. From there, by theoretical analysis, values are extracted, and here we find the beginning of a deontic logic – which, in turn, is tested on actual valuations.

In the literature of deontic logic, credit for the beginning of deontic logic has been given to Ernst Mally. Ernst Mally was Meinong's student in philosophy, especially in the studies of ethical theories. The beginnings of a formal and analytical treatment of obligations and what is permissible is to be found in Meinong's writings, especially in the monograph whose translation is in this volume.

Meinong's writings on value theory were especially influential on Anglo-American philosophers of his time like H. M. Muensterberg, W. M. Urban, H. O. Eaton, J. St. Mackenzie. Later, it was Roderick M. Chisholm who became productively involved with his thoughts.

Ethische Bausteine (**Elements of Ethics**) is a fragment of 66 pages written at the end of Meinong's life. Ernst Mally prepared it for publication in 1921, but it was not published until 1968 when it was included in the third volume of the **Gesamtausgabe,** edited by Rudolf Haller and Rudolf Kindinger.

As mentioned above, **Elements of Ethics** begins with an empirical investigation of the different meanings and uses of the word "value." Meinong determined what things are values for me, the ego; what for the other, the alter. Then he continued with the theoretical question of what things would be values – and corresponding obligations – if they were independent of anyone's specific interest. Following an empirical psychological description of egotistical and altruistic values, Meinong characterized the subject matter of ethics as a theoretical analysis of motives and values and a methodological consideration of ethics as a discipline (including the differentiation of empirical and rational elements within it). Meinong then introduced the Law of Omission, which resulted from a logico-semantical analysis of the description of certain types of actions and their omission which he called value classes, leading to the beginning of deontic logic. According to this law, the omission of meritorious (supererogatory) acts is morally permissible; the omission of merely morally correct actions is morally reprehensible. Meinong represented these relationships schematically by developing a value line analogous to the positive and negative number line, especially considering the line representing modalities. His analysis employed the Aristotelean square of opposites. This will be the subject matter of Section 2, Chapter Seven.

Elements of Ethics, one of the last writings by Meinong, rests on all of the above theories without being obscured by the complicating deliberations of his very late lecture notes. The only exceptions are the so-called incomplete objects. But they are mentioned and used without the impediment of the claims made in connection with them.[12] They can simply be taken as objects of general terms as e.g. names of colors, class names, etc. The fragment incorporates empirical data and induction, conceptual analysis, partially in the form of determining concepts as used in reality and then making them precise for use in a theoretical context. It presents an investigation of the logical relationships between these concepts. It reconciles the apriori approach of **On Emotional Presentation** with early purely empirical approaches. It is Meinong's mature insight that a theory like ethics which applies to actions cannot be purely

---

[12] Complete and incomplete objects, precision objects, and precision concepts are discussed in Section 1, Chapter 3.

apriori. It must also comply with actual beliefs and apply to actions in this life. For this reason the fragment is of special interest. It is by no means descriptive ethics, it is normative but based on empirical data. It does not give a moral system of rules of behavior and attitudes. It is the investigation of various concepts of values, of egoism and the logical relationship between obligations and value classes. Of special interest is this latter part.

Some Biographical Notes

Meinong, who lived from 1853 to 1920, was born in an eastern province of old imperial Austria. His father was a general and of lower nobility, whose title was Ritter von Handschuchsheim. Meinong, as was often the habit among academics of his time, shed the title "von" and "Ritter von Handschuchsheim" and became an ordinary citizen, more respectable in University circles where people of noble origin were not considered to be capable of high intellectual achievement, which was a prejudiced generalization, of course, but a prevalent attitude. Meinong was deeply and idealistically patriotic.[13] He believed in the brotherhood of what he called *Kulturnationen*, civilized nations, and, even though he was, as a follower of Hume, very critical of Kant's thought, he espoused emotionally and intellectually an absolute ethics. He believed that certain objects and actions have an objective value as a property and that this value could be known apriori. He did admit though that his beliefs were difficult to prove, and he admitted that he had not yet succeeded in proving them.[14]

Meinong began his academic education and career as a historian. Under the influence of Franz Brentano and through studies of the English empiricist David Hume, he turned his full concentration to philosophy beginning as a radical empiricist. However, the analysis of psychic presenting experiences, such as ideas and judgments, led him to acknowledge entities which do not exist spatio-temporally and which are not accessible to experience; thus, a gradual transition from pure empiricism to an empirically anchored apriorism took place.

---

[13] See **Philosophenbriefe,** especially those letters written around 1918 and addressed to Anglo-Saxon colleagues.

[14] This will be the subject matter of Section 2 of this book.

During his lifetime Meinong's work was absorbed into Anglo-Saxon philosophy. Russell, of course, comes to mind first, then W. N. Urban in value theory, J. S. Mackenzie, Gilbert Ryle, G. E. Moore, C. D. Broad, and, later, Wittgenstein.

Meinong was an innovator and initiator in many respects. One of these innovations is his value theory. His original ideas have been often attributed to his students in this field, especially to Ernst Mally. But the beginning of their thoughts were with Meinong, as evidenced by his own writing, especially in the appended translation of the fragment **Ethische Bausteine**, now in English, **Elements of Ethics.** Ever since the sixties of this century, both in the United States and abroad, interest in Meinong's and, in general, Austrian philosophy has been steadily increasing among ethical theorists as well as logicians, philosophers of language, and philosophers of mind. Meinong's prolific output, in the context of Austrian philosophy as represented by Brentano, Twardowsky, Bolzano, and Mach, provides a rich source for new thought, revision, and support of existing theories and ongoing scholarly dialogue between English and German speaking philosophers, as evidenced by the numerous articles and books which have been published about Meinong's work.

This book is aimed at audiences from three philosophical disciplines: 1) logic; 2) epistemology, philosophy of mind, and ontology; and 3) general theory of values and ethics. From these the foundation of logic and value theory follow immediately. So my colleagues in areas of these disciplines – especially those interested in the Theory of Objects as providing material for ontologically neutral logics and those working in the field of deontic logic and also general value theory – should find valuable information here.

Meinong's writings on value theory and ethics were all published together in the third volume of the Meinong **Gesamtausgabe.** The edition was prepared by Rudolf Kindinger who also wrote the foreword. The volume contains the following works:

Psychologisch-ethische Untersuchungen zur Werttheorie,
approximately 1884, published 1894

"Über Werthaltung und Wert," 1895

"Für die Psychologie und gegen den Psychologismus in der allgemeinen Werttheorie," 1912

Über emotionale Präsentation, 1916 (On Emotional Presentation, transl. 1973)

Zur Grundlegung der allgemeinen Werttheorie, 1923

Ethische Bausteine (Elements of Ethics), shortly before 1923[15]

About the Translation

It is well known that Meinong's writings are very difficult to read. They are difficult because Meaning was not a good writer. Many of his sentences are virtually incomprehensible. Often parts of a sentence are missing which are essential for its understanding. The translator has two choices, either to render those sentences more clearly in English by forcing an interpretation on them or to leave them as vague as they are in German. I opted for the latter choice. For there is always a possibility that one's own interpretation is not correct. So I leave the reader of the English version with the same difficulties with which I am confronted when I read the German version.

A vocabulary of technical terms follows the translation. It is given in two versions: German to English and English to German.

A Short Overview of the Fragment Elements of Ethics

Values are ideal objects of higher order. They are properties which some objects possess. There are several classes of values: ethical; aesthetic; timological, that is, the value of truth; and the pleasant. In the fragment Meinong first clarifies the concepts of egoistical and altruistic values which are personal values and then proceeds to what is dearest to him, namely, absolute or impersonal values.

One of the most interesting aspects of the monograph is the development of a deontic logic, namely the logical relationships between

---

[15] For the following I will refer to the Foreword written by Rudolf Kindinger, editor of the third volume of **Gesamtausgabe**.

a manifold of value classes. This is done purely theoretically even though he kept in mind the popular use of certain terms and concepts.

In the first five chapters Meinong works out a precise determination of egoism and altruism. So, there are egoistical, altruistic values, and such that are values for a whole group, and such that are impersonal to the extent that the subject for whom they are values does not matter at all. And there are those impersonal values which are absolute and universal. It is irrelevant for whom they are values and who does the valuation. They will be of real importance for any ethical theory.

I have used, to quite an extent, the Documentation Center for Austrian Philosophy in Graz, Austria, which was established around 1984. I gratefully acknowledge the help of Prof. Rudolf Haller and Dr. Reinhard Fabian. The Documentation Center is of special importance because it contains a collection of manuscripts and out-of-print books of many authors whose writings constitute or are influenced by Austrian philosophy. The extent of the collection is outstanding. Likewise my thanks go to Dr. Hans Zotter, the director of the manuscript collection of the University of Graz.

Section 1

Chapter One

Simplification of Meinong's Ontology and Epistemology

Meinong's theories of knowledge and ontology are, at first, second, and third sight, a very complicated subject matter. The Meinongian Universe is a vast and divers one. But in agreement with the mature Meinong, especially the Meinong who had familiarized himself with the new developments in mathematics, especially geometrical axiomatic systems, and logic, this universe can be significantly streamlined[1]. That will be done in the following. But nothing can be discussed concerning his value theory and theory of valuation (*Werthaltung*) without at least explaining his theory of knowledge or theory of presentation and his corresponding ontology before streamlining it. A clarification concerning the term "valuation" is appropriate. It is not very precise. It means the presentation of a negative or positive value by a feeling, it also means the attribution of a positive or negative value to an object[2].

---

[1] Various authors have given versions of a Meinongian universe. Among them are Terrence Parsons, Karel Lambert, Richard Routley, William Rappaport. My version is simplified because it reflects Meinong's ontological attitude at the time of **Elements of Ethics**.

[2] The subject doing the valuation may be different from the value subject who is the person for whom the value object has a value. The subject of the valuation may be someone else. More about that in Section 2.

A.   The Traditional Meinongian Modes of Being

There are, for the main part of Meinong's philosophy, three modes of being: existence, subsistence, and aussersein. Aussersein includes subsistence, subsistence includes existence, not vice versa. Individual objects which occupy space and time, or which occupy time and occur in space, and which are present and are, in principle, perceptible exist[3]. Individuals which existed in the past or will exist in the future subsist. Subsistence is a kind of eternal Platonic being, inaccessible to the senses but accessible to thinking. Some objects which can never exist but which are considered by a good number of people to have some sort of independent being subsist, like natural numbers.

Some properties exist when they are exemplified and some do not exist even when they are exemplified. None of the properties exists when they fail to be exemplified. However, when they are not exemplified Meinong inconsistently assigns, to the same properties, sometimes subsistence and sometimes only aussersein. Aussersein is a lesser mode of being to which every object belongs which neither exists nor subsists. Examples of properties which exist when they are exemplified in existing objects are red, round, being a rose. Examples of properties which subsist even if they are exemplified in existing objects are beautiful, good, useful, guilty, heir, someone's equal. Properties which are exemplified in subsisting objects are of course, subsisting, such as prime number, equilateral, even numbered. They cannot be perceived by our senses but are judged. They are thought objects. Further examples of subsisting properties of existing objects are: the virtue of Mother Theresa, a person's being a rationalist, David Rockefeller's being an heir. In summary: existing properties can be perceived, subsisting properties and properties of merely aussersein can only be thought.

It is important, for the following, to realize that the mature (not the very late) Meinong mostly uses the term "ideal" instead of "subsisting" and "of aussersein." Any object which is taken to be merely an

---

3   The reader is asked to take the notions of past, present, and future here at face value. "Present" is a relative term because it is tied to perception, and perception is tied to living people, at whatever "time." What was perceptible 200 years ago may not be perceptible anymore, and, thus, it does not exist anymore. I have written about the concept of time in **Meinong's Theory of Knowledge.**

object of thought is ideal. Even if it exists but the question of its existence is ignored, then it is ideal. Subsistence and aussersein are merged into ideality. For the following I shall keep only existence and ideality.

B.   Ideal Objects

Any object of thought is ideal, according to Meinong. Existing objects are considered to be ideal objects when their existence is discounted. Our interest is now focused on the difference between existing and ideal objects. We already know that existing objects are at space-time co-ordinates. They are in principle perceptible.

Ideal objects do not have to have those characteristics which belong to existing objects. They may be non-contradictory or contradictory. If they are non-contradictory, they are possible in either of the two senses: 1) they did or will exist, in the past or future; that is ontological possibility, or 2) they are logically possible if they are neither inherently contradictory nor imply a contradiction, nor are incompatible with any other object.

It must be added, though, that the question of the ontology of ideal objects never quit bothering Meinong, especially in respect to values. He was ethically very sensitive and personally believed in the absolute being of values. He believed that an object capable of having a value as a property has a definite value as a property, and that that value acquires a being independent of the object of which it is the property. But the mature philosopher Meinong tried to abstain from ontological assertions in this respect, which is obvious in the attached translation. This does not alter his standpoint that some objects do have a value regardless of people's opinion.

C.   The Elements of Meinong's Universe

The universe consists of anything which can possibly be thought of. Anything which is or can be thought of is an object. "Object" is an all-inclusive term. Objects are divisible into four classes: objecta, objectives, values, and obligations.

Objecta are individual entities, properties, relations (Meinong calls them relata, that is, relations considered without the objects between which they hold; they are multi-placed properties). Individuals may be simple or complex. When they are complex they are constituted of simple or of other complex entities. It is said, then, that they are based on the entities that constitute them. As such they are called complexes and objects of higher order. Examples of such objects of higher order are complex biological organisms, houses, a herd of cows, melodies, sums and products of numbers. Simple and complex individual objects may exist or may not exist. Examples of existing complex individual objects: a neighborhood, a pile of bricks, and the solar system. Examples of non-existing complex individual objects: a nation (as an object generated by people bound together by common laws, constitution, etc.), a symphony, Medusa, the sum 10+5.

The question of existing and ideal properties is answered in the same way as it was done above. Only now we say "ideal," when the traditional Meinong would say "subsisting." Some properties exist when they are exemplified in existing objects such as red, round, being a rose. Some properties are ideal when they are exemplified in existing objects, such as good, useful, guilty, heir, someone's equal. Properties which are exemplified in ideal objects are, of course, ideal such as prime number, equilateral, even numbered. Properties which are not exemplified are ideal.

Relations are multi-placed properties. They require at least two objects in order to be exemplified. Consider the following examples: 1) a child throwing a ball, 2) a hub cap falling off a wheel, 3) 180 being divisible by 12, 4) a woman being the mother of a child. Also here, we can see that some relations may exist (examples 1 and 2 can be perceived), and some relations may not exist (examples 3 and 4) are judged). It is not always clear and indisputable which ones can exist and which ones cannot exist.

Objectives are comparable to Russell's states of affairs, Bolzano's *Satz an Sich*, and Frege's *Gedanken*. They are about objecta or other objectives. That the child throws the ball, that three is smaller than four are objectives about objecta. That it is the case that Napoleon was a great leader, that it is true that little boys are often destructive, or that three is greater than two but smaller than four are objectives constituted of or based on other objectives. The first two are objectives about objectives, the third is a compound objective. Objectives either are the case or are not the case. Meinong also says they are true or false. Objectives can not be perceived and so do not exist. Since objectives require objecta or other objectives in order to be they are objects of higher order.[4] For example, a child throwing a ball is an existing event. The event is an existing complex individual object unfolding in time. It gives rise to an objective corresponding to it. The corresponding objective is about a child's throwing a ball (our language does not allow us to make a clear difference between the names of events and of objectives which are about events). The event simply exists or does not exist. The objective is true or false. There is a very limited decision procedure for the ascertaining of its truth especially for the truth of empirical judgments about objectives. But that is not our problem here.

The third class of objects are values. There are ethical values as good, praiseworthy; aesthetic values as beautiful or awe-inspiring; and so-called timological values as truth. There is also the pleasant. Values and the possibility of their knowledge are the subject matter of the appended translation. Values are not objecta, they are in a class by themselves. The reason is that their presentation (that is, how we mentally present them to ourselves) is completely different from the presentation of objecta, and Meinong got to the classification of objects via the analysis of presenting experiences. The experiences presenting values are feelings, the experiences presenting objecta are ideas.[5] Values are objects of higher order because they need a presuppositional object of which they are a property. They need an object on which they are based. The question with which Meinong will be concerned is if the object on which values are based, must exist or not, and if, once an object is given a value is objectively or necessarily attached to it. This will be discussed in section II chapters four to seven.[6]

Obligations or desideratives, as Meinong calls them, constitute the fourth class of objects. They are analogous but not equal to objectives. They are objects of higher order which require values as 'inferiora' or presuppositional objects on which they are based. They can not be without

---

[4]   Compare **On Emotional Presentation,** p. XXXVII
[5]   Ideas will be discussed in <u>Kinds of Presentation</u> below.
[6]   Compare **On Emotional Presentation,** pp. LIII ff.

their bases. Obligations are the requirement of something valuable to be realized. So, they are also concerned with objectives which are possible. They are not concerned with objectives which are past or present. For I cannot say, when I am working on this chapter, that I ought to work on this chapter because I am doing it already. But as evening is approaching I can say that it is my obligation to feed my dog because the taking care of one's pet is correct and I have not yet fed her, and I am in a position of doing so. Obligations are not concerned with anything which inevitably will be, as for example, in August, September will come. The possibilities with which obligations are concerned are logical possibilities of events which have not occurred yet. If I were out of the country right now then feeding my dog would not be a possibility. Someone might argue, of course, that an objective with which my obligation is concerned is also an ontological possibility. This, although perhaps true, is not something with which the moral theorist is concerned.

D.   Kinds of Presentation

There are two kinds of presentation: intellectual and emotional presentation. Intellectual presentation is of objecta and objectives. It consists of ideas and judgments or assumptions. Ideas present objecta. They are of individuals, properties, relations, or events.[7] Judgments and assumptions present objectives. Judgments are the affirmative presentation of positive or negative objectives. Assumptions are the hypothetical entertainment of objectives. Both contain ideas. Story telling and theoretical deliberations are assumptions. Judgments and assumptions are either true or false if the objective which they present is the case or not, or is true or false. (Meinong varies in his attitude of which is true or false, the judgment and assumption or the objective presented by them. Either way, the relationship is one to one.)

Feelings present values. In the presentation of values an emotional element is found which occurs after the intellectual presentation of objecta or an objective. Even though, as we shall see, there are errors or correctness in valuations, they are not intellectual experi-

_____

[7]   The theory of ideas is quite complicated. See **Em.Pres.** XLI - XLIV and text references therein.

ences. They are emotional, that is, a matter of feeling. They need, however, the presuppositional experience of the intellectual presentation of an objectum or an objective in order to occur. That intellectual presentation is the feeling's psychological presupposition. For example, we see that someone kicks a dog. That is a perception, an intellectual presentation. That presentation gives rise to a feeling of disapproval, of a value feeling "bad." This, in turn, gives rise to the value judgment: kicking a dog is bad.

Obligations are also objects of higher order based on values. Obligations are presented by desires. Desires also require certain judgments and then feelings in order to occur. The presentation of obligations requires psychological presuppositions. For example I judge that my neighbor is sick and without help. This gives rise to the feeling of the goodness of help. This is the psychological presupposition for the desire presenting the obligation to help my neighbor, namely that I ought to help my neighbor. So, if I feel that something is good and I know that it is not yet realized, then the obligation is presented that it ought to be realized. That obligation is presented by an emotional experience which Meinong calls "desire." Returning to the dog example, we would say: the obligation that we ought not kick a dog is presented.

I have spoken repeatedly of objects of higher order and that they are presented. An attempt to work out the mechanism of the presentation of objects of higher order was made by Meinong in respect to intellectual presentation. It should proceed in a parallel fashion with the emotional presentation of values and obligations, but he did not leave us a theory concerning these matters. The presentation of objects of higher order is called "idea production." Idea production, in short words, is the process by which an idea is generated on the basis of ideas which are, in respect to the generated idea, of lower order. Meinong was never able to give a detailed account of that process. I have written about that on two occasions, but the details do not matter here[8]. The melody as an idea is produced by the person who hears the notes which are of lower order in comparison with the melody which is founded on them. The point is, here, that, once the notes are taken in and the process of idea production

---

[8]   In **Meinong on Objects of Higher Order...,** Section 4, Chapter 7, and **Meinong's Theory of Knowledge,** Section II Chapter E.

takes place, the result can only be one certain one. Many ideas are produced ideas. And all ideas of ideal objects of higher order are pro- duced ideas. Also, numbers taken as cardinal numbers are objects of higher order and presented as the result of idea production.

There are other divisions among the vast realm of presentations which need not be mentioned here, because they are not relevant to what is done in this book. I just want to point out that what has been described just now does not exhaust Meinong's traditional theory.

E.   Theory of Objects

The theory of objects has, roughly speaking, the following origin: Meinong began his epistemological investigations by analyzing psychic presentations, i.e. intellectual and emotional presentations: ideas, judgments and assumptions, feelings and desires. Each of these experiences, as presenting experiences, present objects, as was stated above. If we ignore the question of the existence of objects we must still admit that, by their very character, presentations are indeed intending something or are of something, so they have at least what Brentano calls intentional objects; they are objects of our thought. Meinong also calls them "immediate objects" or "pseudo-objects." He calls them pseudo- objects because they are nowhere, neither in our brain nor in an eternal place, but they are there for us, just plainly thought objects. So, when the ontological status of an object of our thought is irrelevant, it is an ideal object[9].

According to Meinong's own theory, it may be objected that existence is the condition of an object's being thus-and-so, its charac- teristics. But that is not so. For example, a property is attributed to Pallas Athena when we say that she is Zeus' daughter. As far as we know, neither Zeus nor Pallas Athena exist or existed. They are ideal objects. We know about Zeus and his daughter by experience, namely by reading or having been told about them. This knowledge about them is about their being thus-and-so, as Meinong would express it. Anything

---

9   Compare Kroon, Frederick W. 'Was Meinong only Pretending?', **Phil. Phenomenol. Res.** 52 (3). In principle I agree with this author. My digression consists in this, that I mainly rely on writings which are later than **On Assumptions,** that is, those writings which concern themselves with the development of modern mathematics and logic.

that can be asserted by us about these two characters – other than repeating what we have read or heard – has to follow from that knowledge or be consistent with it. This is the case with any fictional or even historical character[10]. However, we know from experience about the authorship of the written mythology or about the book from which we know the story, or about how the Greeks worshipped these gods, etc. Any further speculation is either inductive or deductive, depending on how we deal with the information at our disposal.

As mentioned above, the theory of objects evolves when presentations themselves are neglected and only their various objects are studied without consideration of their ontological status[11]. Experience is dealing with existence. Object theory does not deal with existence directly, but it considers the possibility or impossibility of existence.

The nature of an object, its being thus-and-so, neither includes nor implies existence. One cannot say that any individual object whatsoever must be an object of perception[12]. For example, the dragon which was slain by Siegfried, perhaps even Siegfried himself, and Little Red Riding Hood have never been perceived. This merely means that not much can be positively ascertained concerning their existence from the properties of given individuals. But much can be said concerning the possibility or impossibility of existence[13]. An oval triangular object cannot exist in Meinong's universe as far as the universe is subject to the law of the excluded middle. It is only ideal and even impossible, but perhaps Siegfried or the dragon may exist even now. It is conceivable that nothing can be stated why they could not exist right now, even though it is doubtful considering the past and present states of affairs. One cannot say that they cannot exist right now. All of the foregoing statements are object theoretical. They are not statements of experience.

When we consider the boundless realm of objects as objects of thought, then we have the subject matter of the theory of objects. The theory of objects consists in the phenomenological analysis, classification, and description of objects, and that is entirely theoretical.

---

10 Comp. Chapter Four.
11 **Gegstdsth.**, **V** (258).
12 **V** (407).
13 **V** (230).

F.   The Apriori

Meinong makes it very clear that "apriori" does not mean innate but independent of experience[14]. It is difficult to separate Meinong's theory of the apriori from his theory of objects because all object theory is apriori, and all apriori judgments and assumptions are within object theory. The difference lies in this: apriori pertains to presentation and knowledge; object theory pertains to objects. This as a mere theoretical differentiation. There are two ways to study the apriori: 1) as psychology of knowledge, and 2) as object theory[15]. Ad 1): Meinong claims that I know in a way and with a conviction that, for example, black is not white, that the circle is different from the square, that five is smaller than six which cannot be found in experiences such as when I hear, now, a sound or see the moonlight on the tree, or remember a sunrise in the desert. Meinong even excludes experiences like the feeling of pain from certain knowledge even though one cannot be mistaken in that[16]. This standpoint may be disputed by some. Meinong defends his claim by stating that the difference lies in the fact that the four examples of perception and memory lack insight, they are merely a knowledge that something is the case, it is the experientially hitting upon something. Moreover, we can add, they are of existing events. In perception there is a *Vorfinden*, a coming upon, there is no logical ground *(Begründung)*, according to Meinong, no reason, as far as we would know.

The three former examples (black is not white, etc.), however, are judged with insight from the understanding of the objects of my judgment. Meinong calls apriori knowledge *"daseinsfrei,"* "existence-free."

Existence belongs to aposteriori knowledge for it is given in perception or is derived from perception. Necessity of non-existence of contradictory objects – or possibility of existence of those, for example, whose existence has not yet been established, as e.g. ghosts – are the subject of apriori deliberations. Whatever knowledge is based on empirical knowledge and remains anchored to that basis remains in principle empirical although it may contain theoretical (apriori) excursions or

---

14 **V** (380),(256).
15 For 2, see also chapters three and four.
16 **Gegstdsth.**, **V**, (258).

elements[17]. It must be separated from purely apriori knowledge. Empirical knowledge is exclusively of objects which exist (past, present, and perhaps future).

Existing objects are not restricted to empirical knowledge. They stand in various relationships to other existing objects, they are always within some sort of state of affairs or of events. It depends on the ontological status of these relationships or states (events always exist) if they are objects of apriori or aposteriori knowledge. How is their ontological status determined? That can be considered from our manner of knowing them. One takes a class of objects and asks oneself whether those objects can be perceived[18]. Take the example of ghosts again: if there are any, then they are accessible to perception. That most of us, in fact, have not perceived ghosts does not mean anything regarding their existence. But anything that occupies space and time is, in principle, accessible to perception. And ghosts would at least occupy a time interval and occur in space. We must say what we mean by the present tense of "occupy" and then by "space and time." Present is taken, here, relatively as object of perception[19]. If they are perceived they occur at certain space-time co-ordinates. Space-time co-ordinates are understood in the absolute Newtonian sense.

If ghosts exist, they might be observed floating through a room or doing whatever it is that ghosts do. But ghosts may find themselves in different kinds of relationships, they may be observed throwing plates, they cannot be observed being different from other ghosts or having a pact with other ghosts. That is only judged, it cannot be perceived. Extremely basic constituents of the universe, just like ghosts, are not yet perceived but they may possibly be observed, and they exist at some spatio-temporal co-ordinates even though they themselves may not occupy space.

It is already known that priori judgments may contain empirical ideas[20]. That is easily documented in the judgment of difference between two perceived objects. The judging of difference is an apriori

---

[17] Vol. **II** 520 <51>.
[18] Comp. ideal properties of existing objects above.
[19] Comp. **M's Th. of Knowledge,** Time chapter.
[20] **V** (376).

matter. Difference is a relation which does not exist. It is ideal, or, in epistemic terms, it cannot be perceived but can only be thought. It is the result of a thought process[21]. For example, one has to chose between two paths, A and B; one finds A shorter than B by comparison. This judgment of comparison is apriori. On the basis of that knowledge, let's say, a decision for A is made. That there are in fact paths A and B is empirical knowledge. The same is the case with the recognition of a melody. Only the notes are perceived and perhaps the intervals, but the melody itself is an ideal object, an object of higher order based on notes and intervals which is known by thought or by what Meinong calls idea production. Once the notes with their specific intervals are given and idea production takes place, then only one specific idea of a melody can arise, and when it arises the result is apriori and necessary[22].

The difference between apriori and empirical judgments are also found in the degree of certainty of judgments. Only apriori judgments can be certain without qualification. In this respect apriori knowledge is superior to empirical knowledge.[23] If one "knows" by experience, for example, that one's car is red one is never absolutely certain. With many people perception and memory of colors is very unreliable. But one can know with certainty, at times, that if this is the case then that also is the case, necessarily from the nature of the object in question. I ask for the reader's indulgence for the following examples: if my car is red then it is not green or gray; if a planet has a satellite then it has mass; if a man is a bachelor then he is unmarried; if a woman has children then she is a parent; if a blossom is a rose then it is not a carnation. An exception is the drawing of conclusions from apriori premises in a manner which is essentially empirical, i.e. inductive. Meinong's own not-quite-fitting example is: the divisibility of numbers by three according to the divisibility of the sum of its numerals is an empirical conclusion because it is the result of a generalization over results for numbers between 1 and 100.[24] One must make do with such methods as long as a mathematical proof has not been found.

---

21 **V** (239).
22 Compare **M.'s Th. of K.** and **On Objects of Higher Order...** with text references therein.
23 Comp. Kalsi, **M.'s Th. of K.**, Evid. chapter with Meinong references.
24 **V** (240).

Let us consider an object given in perception with a number of properties, its being thus-and-so. From the knowledge of the properties of the given object we can make apriori statements on the basis of the properties and what we have already learned by whatever ways. Take it that a woman in a red skirt is given in perception: she is not a man, she belongs into the class of red skirted objects but not in the class of dice. She does not wear a top garment which is green. She must be of a certain shape and age. She occupies space and time somewhere. A sufficient clarity of the ideas on which those judgments are based is a definite advantage.

As was said above, Meinong believes that the apriori can be studied from two standpoints, the psychology of knowledge (*erkenntnis-psychologisch*) and object theory[25]. And the preceding deliberations are within the psychology of knowledge. Psychological studies, by their nature, are empirical, at least at first before the construction of theories and before theoretical analysis of that which is given in perception. Many psychic events – and the theory of knowledge is interested in presenting psychic events – elude empirical observation, simple instances are ideas considered in isolation from judgments or assumptions in which they occur. Meinong did not state that, but I myself have never been able to present to myself an idea by itself. The reader is asked to think of a brown horse; and what she is thinking, I believe, is a brown horse in a certain situation, painted on canvas, standing in a stable, grazing, or galloping. That is, we are thinking an objective involving a horse. So, ideas, as I see it, must be considered to be theoretical constructs and their study belongs to object theory and the apriori. So does much of psychology. For all presenting experiences are analyzed by Meinong into act and content. The content is that part of the experience which corresponds directly to its object, the act is that part which makes the experience what it is: a judgment when a positive affirmation or denial is made, an assumption when an objective is hypothetically entertained. The same is the case with feelings and desires. None of the parts of the psychological events can be inspected. These parts cannot be empirically exhibited, they are a matter of theoretical analysis or analytical speculation. However, one can be

---

[25] **Erg.** 14ff (251).

aware of one's own judgments, speculations, and valuations as unanalyzed, whole experiences. But their analysis is not empirical.

What we can know apriori and what we can know experientially lies in the nature of the objects of our contemplation and how they are presented. And at this point, we have an inextricable intertwining between the theory of the apriori and theory of objects[26], Meinong believes, we come to be convinced of the apriori character of a judgment through a strong feeling of justification, specifically through the evidence of certainty of individual judgments of relations, and the insight into why the judgment is true[27].

Evidence for certainty is a criterion for apriori knowledge. Evidence is a feeling accompanying judgments. It is a feeling of justification of varying strength. The stronger the feeling, the stronger the evidence. Since evidence is a psychic entity, it may vary from person to person depending upon the knowledge situation of the person. That 245 multiplied by 56 equals 133,720 is of different evidence to different people. If someone uses a calculator and simply accepts the result, it is acceptance without understanding, thus, without evidence. It is not knowledge. If someone fully understands numbers and the algorithm of multiplication and is good in applying it, her feeling of justification is strong because she judges with understanding of why the result is such and not otherwise. It is similar in perception. However, there the possibility of a mistake is never quite excluded. Thus, there cannot be certainty. From a distance we often do not feel sure of what we see or hear; at closer look the feeling of justification concerning what we see becomes stronger but is never as strong as the feeling of justification occurring with judgments of the kind of the recognition of a melody or dissimilarity.

From an object-theoretical standpoint, it can be stated that numbers are ideal, that the rules of multiplication are reducible to numbers and their successors. Any knowledge of them is purely apriori. There are no empirical elements.

---

[26] **Erg.** 81.
[27] Comp. Chisholm **Theory of Knowledge,** 3rd edition.

For example, Meinong claims that the statement that all dropped objects will fall is not as persuasive as the statement that green is different from red[28]. The latter has evidence for certainty, its truth is immediately seen, the dropped object's falling is highly probable because experience, statistics, teaches what has been and what perhaps, but not with necessity, will be. However, if the law of gravity is given as a premise (even though a speculative one) and is taken for granted, then "all dropped objects will fall" follows apriori and with necessity from that premise. Not all apriori judgments are certain. Some are tentative, and their lower evidence is felt.

Meinong also states[29]: Every science is characterized by its subject matter not by its methods because all sorts of methods can be used. A science whose subject matter is exclusively ideal is purely apriori in its mature stage. However, according to Meinong, mathematics, especially geometry, can proceed in part empirically. The subject matter of geometry is geometrical objects which are ideal, and ideal objects are by their nature known apriori. However, the first approach to them may be via observation, drawing, and measuring. That is a simple historical fact. In that case, there are empirical elements in a potentially purely apriori theory.

Meinong goes on to touch on the apriori nature of logical derivations which follow rules which are immediately evident. Meinong addresses G. E. Moore and rejects his equation of rational judgments with derived judgments. This will merely be mentioned, because, in general, Meinong's excursions into logic are often not felicitous, and I will forgo a discussion at this place. He took the rules of deduction as psychological rules of thought, but tautologies and arguments were ideal objects for him.

However, a word may be said about the synthetic apriori. When Meinong was young he ardently rejected the possibility of synthetic apriori judgments in his Kant paper[30]. Later on, this question did not seem to occupy his thoughts. But, then, the very fact of idea production as

---

[28] **V** (378).
[29] **V Gegstdsth**: *Daseinsfreies Wissen*, p. (234)ffff.
[30] **Erg.** pp. 3-24.

a generation of ideas from given material which is not an analysis of given definitions demonstrates that if idea production is in fact apriori then we have synthetic apriori judgments. For from the produced idea of a given melody we judge, "Oh yes, this is the main motif of, say, the fourth movement of Brahms' first symphony." In this case we do not hear the melody first and then analyze the notes out of it. We "synthesize" the melody from the notes. Analyzing the notes out of a melody can be done in an entirely different thought process which is called psychic analysis[31].

In **Über die Gegenstandstheorie im System der Wissenschaften** Meinong speaks, at great length, about geometry. And these discussions are object theoretical. They arose from Meinong's acquaintance with the thoughts of Hilbert, Mach, and Lobachewsky. It is in this period that Meinong realizes that objects of thought are ideal, and it is a mute question to ask if the objects of various geometries are eternally subsisting. This is the reason why, at the onset of this chapter I left out the difficult divisions between various kinds of being and simply divided all objects into existing and ideal ones, which covers the whole ground. And it will not hurt the theory of absolute values, because once an object is given which occasions a valuation it can occasion only one certain valuation, just as it is the case in idea production. The object has a value as a property which is presented by one certain feeling which, in turn, gives rise to one certain value judgment.

In conclusion I will paraphrase passages from a later lecture series, 1917/18. They address the question whether there is any apriori knowledge at all. For example: Take the principle of contradiction or the concept of the uniformity of nature. The first is a regulative principle which cannot even be suggested by experience, the second cannot be gotten by induction[32]. J. St. Mill already discussed the problem of induction and the induction principle.

The late Meinong seems to believe that we apparently cannot arrive at concepts such as the principle of contradiction, the uniformity of nature, or of sufficient reason by experience, they are not given in

---

[31] **Meinong on Objects of Higher Order ...** and **Meinong's Theory of Knowledge.**
[32] **Erg.** 392.

experience nor by induction. By induction we arrive at a statistical notion say of a specific regularity in nature. These thoughts were expressed with the aim in mind to convince his audience and readers that there are concepts which do not have their origin in experience.

Section 1

Chapter Two

Precision Objects and Precision Concepts

A.   Introductory Remarks

The appended translation presupposes the understanding of the term "concept" which has as many meanings as the instances at which it is used. That is why a special chapter is devoted to that term. And the understanding of it is vital for the understanding of Meinong's theory of knowledge and object theory. The early Meinong stood very much under the influence of Hume's philosophy. For Hume, the question of abstract ideas was not even a question. Still there is the problem of abstraction by which the human mind arrives at the recognition of properties as isolated from the complex idea of the individual objects in which properties are exemplified. Abstraction and concept are closely related, as will be seen in the following.

Already in **Gesamtausgabe, Volume I,** "Hume Studien I," Meinong, for lack of a better explanation, makes that nice and somewhat helpless pronouncement that humans are abstracting mechanisms (*Abstraktionsmaschinen*), which is a simple statement for an unexplainable fact with which also J. St. Mill had wrestled. The searching of the young Meinong will be left out here, because the interest must focus on the mature theory which is relevant for his value theory. However, one thing must be said: the question of abstraction and corresponding concepts (ideas) kept haunting Meinong.

First of all, concepts are ideas. Ideas are psychic presentations of a kind of objects which are called "objecta"[1]. Objecta are individuals, properties, relations, numbers, etc., and it does not matter if any of them exist or not, or are ever exemplified. Ideas consist of a content combined with that additional ingredient in psychic presentations which makes it an idea, and ideas cannot be further defined except through their intentions, that is, their objects or their content (which correspond directly to their objects) and as parts of judgments

Concepts are special ideas: they are abstract, that is, their content is not concrete or perceptual. Even though the young Meinong of "Hume Studien I" spoke of concrete and abstract concepts he never provided a differentiation between them, and I take it that there is none. For concrete concepts are perceptual ideas. This leaves us only with abstract concepts, that is, concepts to consider. Concepts are special ideas and have, by their very nature, objects, which are special objects. These objects are the unfortunate incomplete or, rather, incompletely determined objects which have given so much grief to modern philosophers who concern themselves with such matters. These objects differ from individual objects which have infinitely many properties and are completely determined in this, that they consist of only one or a cross section of several properties and are, as Meinong believes, not determined in respect to all the other infinitely many properties which they do not have[2]. This gave rise to all sorts of concerns and speculations by Meinong himself and other philosophers, among whom has been the speculation that incomplete objects are not subject to the law of the excluded middle because of their indeterminateness. I shall not discuss the question at this place. I merely state that the objects which are presented by concepts are completely determined as what they are, namely by their definition. As general objects they belong to a specific type according to Russell's or Carnap's ramified theories of types and are – even without taking Russell's solution into consideration – what Meinong calls later "precision objects." And these objects are what I shall speak about in the following.

---

1 Compare Chapter One above.
2 I have addressed this question in my article "Incompleteness and the Tertium Non Datur" in **Conceptus**, 1995.

Every concept has its content and, with its content, it has an object, its "immediate" object which Meinong also called "pseudo-object." Content and immediate object only differ in this, that content is part of the presenting experience and immediate object is not part of the experience but the intended entity directly corresponding to it. Where and what that entity must be thought to be is irrelevant, it is an object of thought. A concept like any other idea may refer, via its immediate object, to another object which is its remote object. Meinong calls it *"Zielgegenstand."* Example: via the concept and its object "aquatic longhaired sea creature," I may refer to mermaid. Or via the concept and its immediate object "blue moon," I may refer to the remoter object, second full moon in September; or by "Central Europeans," I may refer to Germans.

Different concepts may refer to the same (remote) object or have the same extension, Meinong believes. Example: "freezing at zero degree Celsius" and "consisting of hydrogen and oxygen" are two different concepts which both refer to water[3]. In Meinong's vocabulary it would be expressed thus: These two concepts are each of two different kinds of objects: The immediate objects which correspond directly to their content, and, then, their extension, that is a remote object[4]. The extension of a concept is not the immediate object but a remoter object. Example: The concept "goose" is defined by biologists by naming those properties which all geese have in common and which differentiate them from other animals. That is what is thought by the concept "goose." The extensions of the concept are all geese past, present, and future.

I have emphasized several times before that Meinong does not follow Frege's distinction between sense and denotation. He deals with the psychic presentation, in our case, with an idea or, narrower, with a concept. That concept has a content which corresponds directly to its immediate object (speak "pseudo-object"). It may have a remote object which, then, is its extension. The extension does not have to exist, as has just been shown in the case of past and future geese, or mermaid. The extension may well be ideal objects like all possible triangles are the

---

3 Vol. I, H.St.I, 18.
4 Meinong discussed the question of immediate and remote objects in **On Emotional Presentation**. The reader is referred to that source.

extension of the concept "triangle"[5]. Meinong did not see the problem as a linguistic one; but from the standpoint of psychological philosophy or philosophy of mind, that is, he was concerned with the relation between psychic presentation and its objects.

Quite consistently it goes on: the wider the extension of a concept, the narrower its content. The more general a concept, the more abstract it is. When its content is infinitely large, its extension equals one individual objectum. When its content equals one (a simple concept), its extension is infinitely large (or zero). This follows from the fact that the concrete individual objectum has infinitely many properties[6].

There are abstract concepts of individuals. Meinong's own examples are: the father of this man, the wisest of all men, the most beautiful star[7]. The immediate object of the concept may be described as a set of one element, the intended object is the element itself. The element does not have to exist.

There are cases where the decrease or increase of the content leaves the object of the concept unchanged. That happens when an additional property which all members of a set or species have in common is thought with the concept[8]. The number of the attributes thought in the concept does not indicate whether the concept is general or particular, even though, strictly speaking, as was said above, the content of the concept of an individual can be infinitely large. (Meinong mentioned but did not explain the role of the definite article.) Naturally, the complexity of the content of the concept is relevant for the extension of the concept. According to Meinong, it can, in fact, be a very different matter what we think the extension of a concept is and what it is in reality. That is, the immediate object or pseudo-object of the content may be one thing but its extension may unintentionally be taken to be quite another thing. So, one may be mistaken in that respect.

Meinong admits that if concepts are allowed into one's mental world it must be admitted that the important part of a concept is its content

---

[5] I am aware that I am not in agreement with Marti-Huang **Die Gegenstandstheorie von A. Meinong.**

[6] H.St.I, Vol. I, p.18.

[7] H.St.I, Vol. I, p.25.

[8] H.St.I, Vol. I, p.27.

and that its extension is secondary[9]. In other words, there are concepts which do not have an extension[10]. Examples: unicorn, perpetuum mobile.

B.   Definitions of Concepts

Meinong speaks about conceptual determinations which are neither nominal definitions nor real definitions. They cannot be touched by either the principle of freedom of definition or the adherence to "linguistic use"[11]. Freedom of definition would refer to stipulative or nominal definition[12]. Meinong considers the example of "dirigible" (*Luftschiff*). Its empirical extension is all real dirigibles, its logical extension is all possible dirigibles in the sense of all past, present, and future dirigibles and all ideal dirigibles, which would include dirigibles possibly thought of but never built. This is not quite empirical because the past dirigibles do not exist anymore and the future dirigibles do not yet exist, and the ones which are only thought of never exist. When there are no dirigibles yet except on the drawing board, in formulas, and descriptions, then again we have a concept which is neither totally nominal nor real. It is not quite nominal because it presents something to be brought into existence even though it does not yet refer to anything existing. It is not quite real because there is no existing dirigible yet.

Let us consider the concept of a purely ideal object and its extension. Meinong selects the example "convergent"[13]. It can be understood to have an empirical extension only in an improper sense, as in reality there is nothing truly convergent. Its logical extension is all ideal or possible (free of contradiction) convergences in geometries which contain convergences.

Please note that Meinong makes a difference here between ideal and possible. Ideal objects may be contradictory, that is, impossible. We

---

9   H.St.II., Vol. II, p.86.
10 Comp. **Ann. II.** 273ff.
11 For this and the following refer to **Üb. Möglichkeit und Wahrscheinlichkeit,** page references in the following text.
12 Ibid. p. 69, 70f.
13 Vol. V, **Gegenstandstheorie.**

know that he uses the word "possible" in two senses: 1) free of contradiction, and 2) existing in the past or future. As used here, they both refer to objecta. They also refer to objectives, at least "possible" in the sense of free of contradiction. True objectives are possible, false objectives are not consistent with other true objectives. Thus we would be compelled to say that they are not possible. But all objects of non-contradictory concepts are possible.

This brings us again into the middle of object theory which, for the late Meinong, constitutes his whole philosophy and which, after him, developed into the philosophy of language. (Even moral concepts and relationships are analyzed object theoretically, as in his **Elements of Ethics**[14].)

The object of a concept – that is, the ideal object – assumes a life of its own, in geometry, mathematics, or logic. A lengthy discussion about geometrical concepts follows. It is discussed, for example, what is given in their definitions and what must be added in thought to their definition. In the context of object theory the mature Meinong deals with completely abstract concepts as they appear in the geometries of Riemann and Helmholtz, Lobachevsky, and later, Hilbert[15]. They are not anymore dependent on abstractions from empirically given ideas, they are nominal, completely apriori, constituted by a definition procedure. They are possible on the basis of the theory of assumptions. They are mutually non-contradictory and not contradictory within themselves. That means the basis of perception is entirely removed. It is in this connection that Meinong critically discusses Ernst Mach. Here he finds himself exclusively in the realm of object theory, which again was only possible on the basis of his previous distinction between idea content and object of idea, and by his admission of pseudo-objects or simply ideal objects, without which neither object theory nor even the theories of perception and memory are possible.

---

14   In **Mögl.**, 208. Meinong interestingly enough speaks of the subjectivity of concepts and that they may be even emotionally influenced, a fact which seems quite normal to me. Just think of the definition of concepts of highly controversial subject matters as e.g. obscenity, abortion, political correctness.

15   For the following Vol. V, **Gegenstandstheorie.**

It is stated expressly that concepts correspond to (the infelicitous) incomplete, (please read "general") objects and that (with reference to Höfler) concepts are ideas which correspond to unequivocally determined objects[16]. This points towards precision objects which per se are incompatible with the conception and consequences of incomplete objects[17].

In this context we find the curious statement that concepts are unchangeable but ideas are not. We see that we are in a period of Meinong's thought which is far removed from his younger years. This is theory of objects where Meinong has left psychological philosophy behind and concerns himself exclusively with objects. And once an ideal object is created by definition, it remains there for anyone to think of if she so wishes. What we are to understand is this, once an object has been created by its definition, it is there to stay; and when thought with precision, it is to be thought by its precise concept.

Returning to the difference between the content and object of a concept, Meinong points out that concepts and their objects do not have the same properties. A straight line is straight, but the concept of a straight line is not itself straight. A straight line is not general, but its concept is[18]. Traditional logic (I assume is thinking of traditional Aristotelian logic) is a theory of concepts and, thus, does not belong to object theory but to psychology because it is a theory of thought, according to traditional beliefs. But the new logic, according to Meinong, with its axioms and tautologies belongs to object theory even though the rules of deduction do not belong there, and we can speculate why not. The reader may think of algorithms of arithmetic. They are understood as psychological mechanics of thought. However, logic cannot be excluded from the theory of objects: an argument (form) is the expression of a logical object as are tautologies, contradictions, and contingencies.

---

16   Ibid.(306), (324).
17   The notion of incomplete objects has given rise to much speculation among philosophers. I have dealt with it in the paper "Incompleteness and the Tertium Non Datur," **Conceptus**, 1995.
18   For the following Vol. V, **Gegstdsth.** p.(328), (324).

C.   Concepts and Perceptual Ideas

Meinong says more about concepts and ideal objects. It is formulated by him in **Über die Gegenstandstheorie in System der Wissenschaften**. This is the reason why in this context geometries are discussed, because the theory of concepts and precision objects was developed according to geometrical definitions. So, ethical and moral concepts are to be taken in this sense, as precise ideas of ideal objects.

However, as far as our concrete intuition is concerned (that is concrete or perceptual ideas of geometrical objects), they are imprecise and only approximately correct. Likewise our eyes satisfy, only to a degree, the expectations we have of a precise optical apparatus[19]. This is especially apparent when we consider geometrical objects as objects of perceptual ideas, or even the structure of natural phenomena as e.g. turbulence. However, geometrical objects are foremost objects of the intellect or thought objects. Straightness and parallelity cannot correctly be reduced to equality of objects in perception. To ask, for example, in everyday life, that something not be taken too literally is not to ask an object to become inexact but to adjust the idea to a desired or tolerable lack of exactness[20]. The ideas of many objects are often imprecise because of a natural limitation in us. Ideal objects can be precise, "precise" meaning that all its properties are known, defined, or immediately understood.

The ideas presenting precise objects are concepts which are theoretically determined. Meinong considers, here, essential differences between concept and object. He seems to be doing this in connection with his discussions of Mach who still adheres strictly to the belief in the empirical origin of concepts. The objects of precise concepts are by their very nature and by our intention precise. They are precise because they are constructed to be precise. They are not given in perception or a product of fantasy. In precision concepts the basis of experiences is completely withdrawn. Precision objects like circular and elliptical figures cannot be made precise by any sort of abstraction from perceptual ideas. I take this to mean that by nature our perceptual ideas of circles

---

[19]   Vol. V, **Gegstdsth.** 82.
[20]   For the following Ibid. 83f, 85.

and ellipses cannot be made precise as perceptual ideas. They become precise when taken as objects of mathematical definition within a certain geometrical system. Equality between mathematical objects is precise. It is known by thought and not by perception. Equality between numerals which is known by inspection of the numerals, however, is again imprecise. So, Meinong says, in the history of mathematics and geometry, naturally imprecise objects were replaced by precise objects. It is indeed interesting to note that precision is not the product of abstraction from perception, it is its own genre, it is the product of definition which uses concepts which are independent of perception, even though they may be historically rooted in perception, we may say, rooted in mythology. Meinong, in quoting Alois Höfler, says that theoretical concepts are *"Unterfahren der räumlichen Anschauung mittels des Begriffes,"* which can be roughly translated as "replacing spatial intuition by concepts." And that is a very rough translation, where *"Unterfahren"* means "lifting something from its basis and placing it on another basis," like lifting a car from the ground onto a big jack or lifting a ship from the water onto a dry dock. Thus, it is explained why, in geometry objects are understood quantitatively, even though they ought to have qualitative characteristics. These, however, are not precise. They may not even exist, in the proper sense of the word, and may be beyond our capacity of perceptual ideas anyway. In other words, in geometries we are dealing with ideal objects (or pseudo-objects) which have properties independent of perceptual ideas and existing properties and are precise (i.e. independent of the limits of our perceptual imagination) and which can be thought with precision.

Precision, then, is an object-theoretical concept in respect to objects, and a psychological concept in respect to our thinking those objects. So, geometry is an existence-free science[21]. Addressing Mach, I suppose, Meinong states that, in one respect, "parallel" and "straight line" in concreto are imprecise, but that, in abstracto, they are precise. Such objects have nothing to do with experience except their remote historical origin; they are thought objects; they are ideal and, thus, fall

---

[21]   Ibid. p. 87.

into the domain of object theory and apriori knowledge which suits Meinong just fine.

D.   More about Non-Euclidean Geometry[22]

Meinong speaks with admiration of Hilbert, Helmholtz, Riemann, and Lobachevsky. He had to face two developments in mathematics: 1) the new axiomatic methods of Hilbert, Riemann, Lobachevsky, etc., and 2) the empirical attitude of Mach, continued later by Moritz Schlick.

Meinong spends much time writing about parallel lines. The point of that discussion is probably that, in the language of Euclidean geometry, it is simply inconceivable that parallel lines intersect or that Lobachevsky can speak of parallel angles or Helmholtz of straightest lines. Meinong gives the impression that the word "parallel" should be reserved for Euclidean geometry, out of reasons of feeling for language. But these controversies by themselves are of no relevance here anymore. The point is that geometry deals with objects of its own creation, but objects they are and they lend themselves to analysis which is purely apriori. These objects are not the result of abstraction anymore; they do not claim to represent or be part of reality. They deal with space, but with space which may not remotely resemble any real space.

Anyway, the space of our perception, as many (among them Moritz Schlick) pointed out, is rounded. It is not the space of our physical and geometrical theories, which is three-dimensional: straight up, down, and sideways. Already Euclidean geometry deals with space which is not the perceived space. The spaces of geometry are ideal (pseudo-objects)[23]. They are of psychological interest insofar as they are thought, and thought itself is an object of psychological, that is empirical, analysis. But this part is the only empirical part in the matter. As in mathematics, geometry receives its purely apriori character by dealing exclusively with objects which are generated by definition. The primitive terms of definitions can be anything one

---

22   The reader is referred to **Gegstdsth.**, V, (283) to (308).
23   **Gegstdsth.**, 100.

chooses. (I remember vaguely a Hilbert expression that geometry deals only with logical relationships, and that it does not matter if its objects are beer mugs and coasters or points and lines.)

Concerning Mach, Meinong's primary reference is Mach's book **Erkenntniss und Irrtum**. Before Meinong enters into the discussion of Mach he expressly states[24]: "... I will not deny the possibility of a geometry which bases its statements on observation and experiment as also physics does." This is, Meinong says, what some of his contemporaries like to call "natural geometry." Accordingly, when one talks about apriori knowledge in mathematics, one must keep in mind the difference between the empirical origin of ideas and empirical justification of judgments. The historical origin of ideas adds nothing to the question of apriori knowledge. Meinong picks up Mach's statement: "... we exert logical power *(Herrschaft)* only over concepts whose contents were determined by us." Meinong takes exception with the word *"Herrschaft"*: when someone has an insight into something, he does not feel like exerting power over it but, rather, has a feeling of understanding. He may be free of a compulsion which one feels when one is confronted with a fact and does not understand it, as is the case in the perception of any object just being there, a so-called "brute fact." Of course, mathematical concepts arose from our dealings with reality, in this Meinong concurs with Mach, and that is the history of man's intellectual development. But even in the actual measuring of a line with a ruler or tape, which seems to be so very perceptual and experiential, the apriori component, namely that of comparison, is ignored by Mach.

Our dealings with reality do not immediately produce mathematics, which treats of objects that do not at all occur in reality: straight lines, constant curves, irrational or imaginary numbers. Seen from its apriori side, mathematical knowledge is certain; in that case it cannot come from empirical induction[25]. If one sets out to check whether a number is divisible by three and actually divides it, one engages in an activity of applying the algorithm of division and ends up with a result. If one fully understands the algorithm and has not just memorized it

---

24   For the following refer to **Gegstdsth.**, V, (268)ff.
25   Ibid. p. (272).

apriori and with certainty. The result of a mindless application of a memorized algorithm is not knowledge at all. It is a blind trust in the correctness of the algorithm[26].

The geometries and their various axiomatic systems may be logically consistent and are not meant to represent real space. Objects are introduced by definition and are thought by precise concepts and deal, thus, with precise objects which are ideal, and consequently objects of apriori knowledge. The fact that the axiom of parallels does not hold in them or that Euclidean geometry can do without that axiom does not really concern parallels themselves. For, first, parallels belong, if they "occur" at all, in Euclidean geometry; and in that geometry there are, in fact, two straight lines of equal distance from each other which never intersect. That is the concept of parallel lines. Therefore, to deny this, within Euclidean geometry, will amount to a contradiction with the concept itself. It appeals to our intuition, as all of Euclidean geometry does, even though it does not represent the space of our perception. In our culture and psychologically speaking, Euclidean geometry is easier to understand. But its objects are as abstract and artificial as the objects of other geometries. So, all geometries, including the Euclidean one, are entirely existence free, ideal, and, thus, apriori. Geometry, and also mathematics, are special theories of objects, their objects being given by axioms and definitions. Meinong refers with special admiration to Hilbert, whose work in geometry frees it from any special geometry and brings it toward a general geometry or general theory of objects.

In the end, for Meinong, mathematics and geometry are part of object theory which deals with its material in a purely apriori manner. He sees his theory as an all-inclusive theory of apriori thought. "Object theory has the task to accomplish for the totality of objects what mathematics did accomplish with a segment of objects and what mathematics will accomplish with a much larger domain of objects"[27]. Another quote of the same work: "F. H. Jacobi said of mathematics that it is "'the doctrine of objects which are understood in and by them-

---

26 Meinong discusses these cases in respect to evidence. See Schubert Kalsi **Meinong's Theory of Knowledge**, evidence chapter with Meinong references.

27 **Gegstdsth.** 101, also for the following.

selves.' Perhaps we can say with greater justification: 'Object theory is the doctrine of that which is understood in itself.'"

Why object theory did not survive as a discipline is an interesting question. It probably did not survive because its task was appropriated by phenomenology, philosophy of language, analytic philosophy in general, logic and relation theory, and the philosophy of mathematics.

Section 1

Chapter Three

Incomplete Objects and
Their Problems

A. Introductory Remarks

By now, the reader knows that Meinong's universe consists of everything one can possibly think of. This includes contradictory objects, including contradictory objectives. But the universe with which science and moral theories deal is limited by the law of the excluded middle or the tertium non datur. Many contemporary philosophers, and occasionally Meinong, take it that the Meinongian universe is one in which the tertium non datur[1] does not hold.

This chapter addresses the question of the tertium non datur as it was once raised, and is still discussed, in the context of the Meinong-Russell controversy and in ontologically free logics. It is claimed that the TND does not hold under certain conditions.

The whole question arose through Meinong's theory that there are incompletely determined objects which are "open" enough to allow for contradictory properties. I mentioned this briefly in the previous chapters. For example, he says that a triangle as such is equilateral and not equilateral, a viewpoint which was already expressed by Locke[2]. In

---

[1] Hereafter referred to as TND.
[2] This point will be discussed at length below.

the preceding chapters I have avoided speaking of incompletely determined objects because I hold this concept to be extremely problematical.
But as Meinong introduced it I must address the question, at last.
(Simply speaking, incompletely determined objects are universals,
referred to by general terms of all kinds.)

Russell insisted that TND holds universally in his restricted
universe; Meinong states that it does not hold in his unrestricted
universe. In connection with the tertium non datur the question of
existence, subsistence, and lack thereof received its importance, and, it
was claimed, the range of the TND only extends over objects which
either exist or are (logically) possible. This claim by itself is not
objectionable.

TND does not hold for impossible objects obviously, i.e. those
which are inherently contradictory, as the oval triangle. The late
Meinong says sometimes that it also does not hold for other objects which
neither exist nor are impossible and which have only *aussersein* [3], a
kind of pseudo-being[4], which is a third kind or way of being of those
objects which are incompletely determined.

Meinong's standpoint – which can be understood as either
ontological or semantic or both, depending on how he is read – will be
examined. It will be shown that, on the basis of his own epistemology
and consequent ontology, his opinion cannot be supported. TND fails to
apply only if we intend it to fail, and I am speaking of a universe which
is determined by the analysis of our presenting experiences. That is the
crux of the whole discussion. This chapter will examine the incompleteness of objects and will show that it is a result of choice of thought
reference or linguistic attitude if you will.

In spite of my having simplified Meinong's universe as consisting of existing and ideal objects, I will state quickly again Meinong's
theory of existence and subsistence. They are ways or kinds of being
which, in modern literature pertaining to the Meinong-Russell contro-

---

3 "Aussersein" will remain untranslated and will be adopted as a technical
term by the English language as it has been done in contemporary
Meinong literature.

4 "Incompleteness and Fictionality in Meinong's Object Theory," **Topoi**,
Vol. 8, 1989.

versy, have been discussed but have not been fully explained. Two examples are papers by K. Lambert[5] and R. Haller. Both address the question of incompleteness of objects and its relevance to the applicability of the principle of the excluded middle or tertium non datur. Lambert does not explain what makes complete objects complete in comparison with so-called incomplete objects; and he does not make clear what non-subsisting objects are. The same holds for Haller. It seems to me that these authors also do not make a clear distinction between existing and subsisting objects.

B. Existence

It is essential to keep in mind that Meinong's ontology depends on the analysis of what he calls "presenting experiences." It is for this reason that he refused to accept Russell's theory of types which would, in fact, provide a solution to the problems discussed in Lambert's and Haller's papers. Russell's theory of description refers to language and objects; Meinong's theory refers to psychic events and objects presented by them. Presenting experiences, by their very nature, are of something, they are without exception intentional, they, without exception, refer to an object of some sort or another. It is the intention which makes the object.

At first glance the theory of existence seems to be quite unproblematic. Everything which occupies space-time coordinates exists. Even if the object itself is not occupying space, it must at least be located in or traveling through space. Everything which is the object of a true description in Russell's sense exists. Everything which exists must be an individual object, that is, everything which can be the subject in a proposition containing first order predicates[6].

Napoleon, I think, did occupy space-time coordinates. We would say that he existed but does not exist anymore. Existence involves time, that is, time as the order of past, present, and future; and existence is tied to the present. The discussion of what present is goes beyond the scope of

---

5 As Haller writes in "Unmögliche Gegenstände, eine Untersuchung der Meinong - Russell - Kontroverse," **Conceptus**, Vol. 11, 1977.

6 There is a way in which properties and relations can exist with or in an object which is called "implexive being," but I shall leave that aside.

this chapter. However, one can say in Newtonian language that present is that which, in its objective time interval, also occupies space. Or expressed in relative terms: anything exists which is in a – in principle verifiable – causal relationship with other objects. Present is not exclusively a matter of time indices, it is also a matter of possible perception. What can I say about existence which is acceptable to us for the purpose of this chapter? I only manage to be circular by saying that everything which occupies space and time at present and which is, in principle, perceptible exists, whereby it remains unanswered what present is[7].

Again, existing objects are what Meinong calls completely determined. That is, for all imaginable properties and relations they definitely have them or do not have them, or stand in them or do not stand in them, respectively. That is, the TND applies to them. The requirement of verification does not matter here.

We all agree that Napoleon and Caesar and the sandwich I just finished eating do not exist anymore. Somehow, for some psychological reason, it seems difficult to dismiss the two people into utter non-being, so at least said Meinong speaking as historian. It is easier with the sandwich; it will not have the influence on the path of history as the two people had, at least not the sandwich I just ate. It may have been different with Caesar and Napoleon. What do we do, then, with Napoleon and Caesar, or even with other things which are not living organisms such as destroyed buildings? We assign to them another kind of being which is called "subsistence." It is that kind of being which Plato's eternal objects had, timeless and changeless, even though he would not call their being properly existing. They remain eternally subsisting individuals with eternally fixed time indices. However, in the context of this book, subsistence is absorbed into ideality, moreover into logically possible ideality.

C.   Existence and Ideality

Since, for Meinong, all thought is presentational (or intentional, in Brentano's terms), all thought is of something, of an object in the most

---

7   Meinong's theory of time comp. my **Meinong's Theory of Knowledge** (see Meinong references therein).

general sense of the term. That object as such has some kind of being. It either exists or is ideal (remember that I have drastically simplified Meinong's ontology in the first chapter[8]). I who am writing this exist right now; when I shall be dead I may continue as a thought object – if anyone cares to think of me – with eternally fixed time indices as part of my concept, but now changeless, free of any changing, temporal determination. Numbers are of that kind but without time indices, likewise imperceptible relations, such as that of equality or being an heir of an estate. They cannot be perceived but only thought. So-called objects of higher order (which are everything except simple, non-complex individuals[9]) are ideal, such as nations or melodies which are based on people and their conventions or on notes and intervals respectively. A nation or melody cannot be perceived by our senses, they become known after our sense perception of the objects on which they are based took place. We, so to speak, generate their ideas or concepts, we synthesize the given sense data or other information into the idea of nation or melody[10]. Again, ideal objects may be either possible or impossible. Also here we have inclusivity. Incomplete objects are what we may call universals or general objects. They, by themselves, are ideal.

Now the question is by what criteria do we differentiate between a complete or rather completely determined object and an incomplete or incompletely determined object? And that is precisely the question which Meinong does not answer consistently; and the determination of the TND's failure to hold depends on the answer to that question. We must now turn our attention to the question of complete and incomplete determination.

D.   Complete and Incomplete Objects

Meinong's theory, as far as it can be made out, is as follows: "Complete objects" is the short expression for "completely determined objects," and "incomplete objects" for "incompletely determined

---

8   Compare with Haller's paper, p. 65.
9   See Meinong's "On the Psychology of Complexes and Relations," in **A. Meinong on Objects of Higher Order**.
10 I am referring mainly to **Über Annahmen II**, paragraph 46 (English **On Assumptions**).

objects." Meinong states that TND holds only for complete objects or for propositions whose subject terms name a complete object. An object is completely determined if, for any given property or relation, it is the case that it either has that property or does not have it, and stands in that relation or does not stand in that relation. It does not matter whether we are, in fact, able to ascertain whether it has that property or stands in that relation. Verifiability is a problem separate from these questions. We would expect that, for any given object, it can be decided if it is completely determined or not. We will see in the following whether that is really the case, according to Meinong's theory. Meinong believes that any existing and possible ideal object is completely determined. We do not have any problems with existing objects, i.e. individuals, even when they do not exist anymore. Caesar ate breakfast on July 10, 1888 or he did not. Well, as far as we know, he did not. He did or did not like gold ornaments. I do not know which was the case, but I do know that one of the alternatives had to hold.

When we turn to ideal objects, the matter becomes more murky. Ideal objects may be anything including impossible objects. At this juncture Meinong retreats to examples, and when his written work is scrutinized one finds that, at one time, one thing is taken to be complete and, at other times, the same thing is taken to be incomplete. Completeness is also ascertained by the number of what Meinong calls "*konstitutorische*" properties which in general has been translated with "nuclear" properties (e.g. Findlay, Lambert, Haller). Nuclear properties make an object what it is. I have not been able to determine in the mentioned literature what kind of properties they are and if they are limited to any kind of type or order. Existence or being completely determined are not "nuclear" properties of an object, so everyone states. Accordingly, being complete or incomplete are also not nuclear properties. An individual, then, is completely determined at least by all the innumerably many first order properties which it has or fails to have. For example, to be red is a nuclear property of a certain rose, but color is not. The same holds of relations: "Jack eats a potato" is, if true, a nuclear relation holding between Jack and a certain potato. But being a two-place relation is not a relation which holds between Jack and the potato. This can be instinctively accepted by us. But what about general objects like classes, properties, relations, numbers, geometrical objects? When are they complete and when are they not? For some must be complete because there are some which are claimed to be possible for which, consequently, the TND holds. Here is where Meinong resorts to examples to which he does not consistently stick[11]. He follows the lead of Locke who believed that triangle as such is neither isosceles nor equilateral, nor scalene. Triangle is undetermined in respect to these properties. And one must understand why he believed that, at least sometimes. For Meinong himself, at one occasion, equilateral triangle is not possible ideal, whereas at another occasion it and rectangular triangle are possible ideal (always remember our reduction of subsistence to possible ideal, and of aussersein to including the impossible ideal[12]). What is the difference between these two triangles? They are both universal objects of the same order, taken from Euclidean geometry. One can say correctly about the equilateral triangle that its angles are equal, and of the rectangular triangle that the sum of the angles at its hypotenuse is 90 degrees. So essentially they are of the same kind and order, and we can ask now: why would Meinong say at one time that an equilateral triangle is possible ideal and at another time that it is not? It seems to me that this depends on how one looks at the object. And how one looks at it depends on Meinong's theory of presentation. He does not say so, he does not say anything, neither do his various interpreters. But the answer lies in that.

First, however, some summarizing statements must be made about complete determination. The following can be said in agreement with Meinong, as far as I can make him out:

1. Generally speaking, an object is completely determined if and only if of any given (nuclear) property or relation it is true either that it holds of it or that it does not hold of it.

2. A nuclear property (relation) is,

---

[11] e.g. **Ergänzungsband**, 376, fourth lecture on epistemology 1917-1918, **Über Annahmen II**, 71, 239 (1910), all volumes together appeared as **Gesamtausgabe**, Graz, 1973-78.

[12] **Über Möglichkeit und Wahrscheinlichkeit (Mögl.)** 69 (1913), **Über Annahmen II (Ann.II)**, 239.

- for individuals, all properties (relations) of the first order, or their negations.

- for general objects O_i, at least all properties (relations) of the next higher order P_{i+1} (or their negations) which it has or which can be derived from the concept of the object[13]. Nuclear properties are those properties whose presence determine the completeness of objects.

3. The concept of an object is linguistically determined by the definition of its name. The concept itself is a precise idea or precise psychic presentation of that object. The object of a concept is called by Meinong "*Präzisionsgegenstand* ," which means precise object. (The reader is referred to precision objects in Chapter Three.)

4. Of any given object there ought to be a method to check whether it is completely determined or not. So far it can merely be stated that if an object is either an individual or a precision object it is *per definitionem* completely determined.

5. Idea or precise psychic presentation of that object is a concept. The object of a concept is called by Meinong "*Präzisionsgegenstand,*" which means "precise object." (The reader is referred to precision objects in Chapter Three.)

- TND does not hold for impossible objects (e.g. round square, oval triangle); therefore, they can be counted among incomplete objects. Impossible objects are a subclass of incomplete objects for which the TND does not hold.

6. Primitive terms are not defined; they hold a special position in any language, are immediately understood, and precise. Therefore they name complete objects, and the TND holds for them. Examples: the relations of difference and equality[14].

---

13 This follows from writings of the young Meinong on the apriori, e.g. about Kant's analytical judgments in **Erg.**, and on concepts in **Gegstdsth.**

14 This is nowhere explicitly stated in Meinong's writings. But comp. **Kausalität, Vol. V,** (494).

E.   Critique of and Suggestions
Concerning Meinong's Theory

I will return to equilateral and rectangular triangles. As objects of Euclidean geometry, they can be defined thus: 1) Areas are two-dimensional objects whose boundaries are three straight intersecting lines all of which are of equal length, 2) Rectangular triangles are two-dimensional objects whose angle opposite the hypotenuse measures 90 degrees. Any statement which can be derived from that definition by previously accepted axioms and rules of deduction is true of the triangle. So it can be said that all angles in equilateral triangles measure 60 degrees. Nothing can be said about the length of its sides. Statements of that kind cannot be made. They do not involve nuclear properties. There is no specific length unless given for purposes of constructing that triangle on paper. But that is not the equilateral triangle as an abstract object of higher order. Therefore any statement about the length of its sides is inapplicable. It does not have a color as nuclear property, there-fore the alternative "it is red or it is not red" is not given. It is an object of higher order, so lower order predicates are not predicable of it. It does not have weight, etc.; it is not cubic or 200 years old. All statements which do not follow from its definition or which contain predicates of an order lower than is appropriate are meaningless or simply false. So, it can be shown that each of these two triangles is completely determined in respect to its nuclear properties. Why, then, would Meinong say, at one time, that it is incomplete? According to some of the late Meinong's beliefs, classes, species, sets are incomplete, and he states that without explanation[15]. But if, in fact, they are precise objects of precise concepts, then they are complete according to the criteria given above and accord-ing to the theory of precision objects, and the TND holds for them[16]. He is wrong from this standpoint. However, there is a curious way in which they may be taken to be incomplete which follows from his theory of presentation to which I now return.

---

[15] **Erg.** 256.
[16] Compare Chapter Two.

F.   Meinong's Theory of Presentation

He speaks of "as what objects are intended[17]." In order to make
that clear, it must again be pointed out that Meinong's theory of seman-
tics does not make the distinction between meaning and denotation. For
him, there is the presenting experience which may be either an idea
presenting individuals, properties, relations, abstracta, etc., or a judgment asserting (denying), or an assumption, respectively, entertaining
a proposition which, however, is called "objective" by Meinong. An
objective is not a meaning but more akin to a state of affairs. A judgment is true if the state of affairs obtains, false if it does not obtain. I will
ignore feelings and desires and their objects at this place. They have
been discussed and will be discussed again in the following chapters.
Of course, ideas or their corresponding objects are named and Meinong
is aware of the difference between idea and name, but the point is that he
concentrates his analysis on ideas and not on names.

As was stated earlier, according to Meinong each presenting
experience consists of two parts, act and content. The content is that part
of the experience which corresponds directly to the presented object; the
act is that part of the experience which makes the experience what it is,
namely an idea or a judgment (or assumption[18].) If I think of elephant
then the object of that idea is precisely what I think of at that moment.
Meinong would say when I think of an elephant as an individual but
intentionally as an undetermined and vague object – whatever that may
be – then the object of my idea is incomplete and, thus, has only aussersein. I deny implicitly that it is determined in respect to all nuclear
properties which individuals by their nature do possess, or I may want to
intend an elephant which explicitly only has a few of the elephantine
properties or which is intended to be open in respect to these properties
and even to have contradictory properties. On the other hand, one can
say that, following Meinong's own theory of presentation, either an
individual elephant is presented who is automatically completely

---

[17] **Über die Stellung der Gegenstandstheorie im System der
Wissenschaften (Gegstdsth.)**, 121 (1906/07), also **Erg.** 376.

[18] **On Emotional Presentations (Em. Pres.),** Chapter 1 (1917), The
Hague, 1972. Translated by. M.-L. Schubert Kalsi. See references
therein.

determined as an individual even though I cannot know or think of all its properties, or the class of elephants is presented which is given by the definition of the term naming the class. But that is then what it is, no more nor less. This object may correspond to something existing or merely ideal, possible or impossible. But its completeness depends on what is intended. So, triangle in general is not isosceles, not scalene, not equilateral, etc. If "triangle" is considered as a specific class of triangles, then it is either isosceles or scalene, etc., triangles. But the class of those classes has neither of those properties. It is a precision object and as such is complete. As was mentioned before, Meinong followed in Locke's footsteps when he expressed these curious thoughts, and he did say so[19].

The purpose of the above is to explain Meinong's peculiar distinction between complete and incomplete objects. In some of his examples of presentation and its object he, in fact, states that its possibility depends on what is intended.

At one place Meinong writes that a square may have equal or unequal diagonals if I do not insist that it should be able to exist or be possible[20]. How can we understand that? How can a square possibly have unequal diagonals? My answer is, if the immediate object of that idea (which is definitely not a precision concept) is just an object intended to be incomplete or contradictory (like the just mentioned elephant), then it may have whatever I want it to have, even contradictory properties. In that case I wanted to think of an incomplete object for which the TND does not hold. But it is noteworthy that I wanted to intend an incomplete object. Not far in space and date from this statement, Meinong made another statement which is also quite baffling[21]. There

---

[19] An idea and its (immediate) object may be used to intend something other than that immediate object. This is a theory which Meinong developed in **On Emotional Presentation.** Then the immediate object via which another object is intended is called "auxiliary object." I may think of "that thief," thereby intending a specific person who was identified as having stolen my daughter's car. According to Meinong all these (immediate) objects of presentation are incomplete because they for themselves only are as what they are thought of, but they fulfill the function of referring to another object which, in turn, may be complete or not. All in all they follow the same pattern as other objects do.

[20] **Erg.** 257.

[21] **Erg.** 376.

Meinong says that he does not see why the diamond sphere of one km diameter should not be completely determined. What is the difference between that diamond sphere and the square? Neither one exists. Meinong does not say why that diamond sphere should be completely determined. It may be undetermined in respect to color, clarity, location. We can find the answer by considering as what it is intended, namely in the way of its presentation. If that sphere is completely determined, one must have two things in mind, either an (empty) class, an abstract object which is presented by a concept, or a fictional individual object. In the first case we have the class diamond and whatever we must think with diamond, e.g. of a degree of clarity and color, and reduce that concept to spherical and one km diameter. That is the precise object. I conclude, just as above, that anything which can be derived from its concept is true. Any lower order property cannot be attributed to it. (This point must be refined, but it will suffice, I think, to refer the reader to the ramified theory of types which does apply to objects of presentation.) This concept does not differ in any way from that of the equilateral triangle discussed above. It is not internally contradictory and has precisely those properties which are explicitly and implicitly contained in its concept. It does not matter that the sphere may be an empty class. For we are talking of an abstract object, given by a concept which is, therefore, complete and possible ideal.

If I intend the diamond sphere to be an individual, then I am intending a fictional object and as such I may want to intend it as being incomplete in respect to its nuclear properties, and I, therefore, intend it not to be subject to the TND. And so we have arrived at the question of fictional characters which in itself is quite interesting. If I think of an individual, fictional or not, i.e. an object of zero order, without the explicit stipulation that it be incomplete, then it is *per definitionem* complete in respect to its nuclear properties even though I may not know anything about most of its properties. Since it is complete, the TND applies to it and it does not have contradictory properties. In this they are not much different from Napoleon, which perhaps indicates the answer to the question concerning the ontological difference between fictional objects and those of the past whose past existence nobody can guarantee.

Napoleon may be an invention of historians. No one can prove that he is not.

Meinong presents us, here, with a phenomenological determination of objects by analyzing the objects of presenting experiences. If an intended individual actually exists or not cannot be decided. None of the methods discussed here is of any help. For ascertaining existence we need to consult his theory of perception and evidence[22]. Of course, it is understood that "existence" is taken in the sense described above, as spatio-temporal and in principle perceptible.

In his theory of objects Meinong does not speak any more about subsistence but about ideality, as was mentioned frequently in the previous chapters. Ideality includes subsistence and aussersein without discrimination. This, of course, obliterates the applicability of the TND and makes an indication of the limits of the universe of discourse mandatory or at least requires the introduction of operators distinguishing between objects subject to TND and those which are not.

We must be very careful when Meinong uses the terms "complete" and "incomplete." It is best to understand them as "general." For his own theory of these objects is quite inconsistent.

---

[22] Comp. Schubert Kalsi, **Meinong's Theory of Knowledge,** chapters II and VI, Martinus Nijhoff, 1987.

Section 2

Chapter Four

Absolute Values

When I simplified Meinong's universe so drastically, I remained painfully aware that this was following a Meinong of a period when he was intensely occupied with modern science and mathematics and logic. It is not all of Meinong. For Meinong the being of eternal or subsisting objects was very important. This is true especially in respect to values and obligations. He believes that ethics is not relative but eternal and absolute, except strictly personal values and those clearly dictated by a communal code.

According to Meinong, there are four classes of values: the pleasant, beautiful, true, and good. In this book, as in the translation of **Elements of Ethics**, the focus is on moral values, the good and the bad, which are a part of ethical values in a wider sense which cover the correct and obligatory, praiseworthy and reprehensible. I will not insist on a clean differentiation between these two classes. For the sake of simplifying his procedure, Meinong narrowed the field of his analytical investigation to moral values, that is, the values of objects which are called morally good or morally bad. From there the analysis can be generalized over the other values classes.

It is very difficult to write about absolute values even with the assistance of Meinong. For at closer scrutiny his writings involve a lot of wishful thinking. The analysis of values which are assumed to be absolute shows that much has to be assumed before they can be exhibited or found.

So I begin quoting Meinong in order to show the strength of his conviction: "But as there are laws for the correct deriving of conclusions so there are laws for correct desires[1]." Desires are the presentations of obligations. Obligations are based on values as their presuppositional objects and will be spoken of later. But the point is here, that there are value judgments which are just as reliable as conclusions from valid arguments, and they are apriori. So Meinong believes that as there are valid arguments regardless if anyone ever thinks of them, so there are obligations regardless if anyone ever recognizes them. And the knowledge whether a given object has a value or not can eventually be obtained. Meinong arrives at the following result: We have knowledge expressed by judgments whose predicate is the proper object of an emotion and whose subject is the presuppositional object either in fact or as possibility. And those judgments are apriori and certain.

Absolute values are properties which adhere to an object which may exist or which may just be ideal. When it is stated by Meinong that no one will disagree that love, justice, truthfulness are values, one must ask: are they properties of objects or relationship between objects which may be real or ideal whenever or wherever they may show up in the universe[2]? If values are bound to objects then they arise with the appearance of the objects. For the just enumerated values are bound to the occurrence of human beings. They are only absolute as long as humans exist or are logically or ontologically possible. This means that values arise with their presuppositional objects. This is in agreement with Meinong's theory of objects of higher order which, for their being, need objects on which they are founded. However, once an object of higher order arises, it remains there as a possible ideal object even if its foundation is taken away. So "all incidents of benevolence are good" would mean as much as the universal proposition "if there are benevolent acts, then they are good," and their goodness does not depend on the benevolent act. Even the act, hypothetically considered, is good.

---

[1] For the following see **Em. Pres.** pp. 113f, 121, 122.
[2] Ibid. p. 119.

Let us look at the overworked example of similarity. In order for the relation of similarity to arise there must be objects on which it is founded, objects which are similar. Once these objects are given so is their similarity. Now, if there are no existing similar objects, that is, if they are only ideal or thought objects, then the similarity still holds between them and is eternally so. What does this analogy mean for values? Values as objects of higher order need at least one presuppositional object in order to "arise." It does not matter if that object exists or is ideal. Values are not created by the experiences which merely present them, namely feelings[3]. Even though absolute values need a presuppositional object, they do not need a subject for whom they are a value. They are "relation-free." This also makes them impersonal. So, absolute, relation-free, impersonal values are the same. However, it was through the phenomenological analysis of personal values that Meinong eventually arrived at impersonal values. For personal values, that is, objects which have value for a specific person or persons, can easily be empirically established by observation or polling. The road to absolute values leads through empirical fact finding. In a way, it is a polling method, or rather a method utilizing the description of actual valuations. Meinong compares this with the relationship between physics and the external world. Physics is not dealing with phenomena, nor with the "thing in itself," but it tries to go beyond phenomena to that which produces them[4]. According to that analogy, value theory does not deal with what people do value but with the explanation of or reason for valuation. There are many motives for valuation. Among egoistical and altruistic valuations, there are impersonal or absolute valuations neither considering one's own nor other people's benefit. Examples of such values would be the respect for the nobility of moral law or for the goodness of a person's intentions.

A distinction is made between potential and actual values: the former is in principle existence-free; the latter includes existence of the presuppositional object of the value in question[5]. This does not interfere with the description of absolute values. For I owe loyalty to my existing

---

3   Ibid. p. 129 p. 135.
4   Ibid. p. 138, **Vol. V**: Erfahrungsgrundlagen, par. 18.
5   For the following see **Grundlegung**, pp. 129, 132, 134.

friend but also to any potential friend. When there is no objectum, neither existing nor ideal, there is no value concerning it. Values are predicates of objects regardless if they exist or are ideal. Values are not individuals, they are properties of a special kind, namely those which are presented by feelings.

Tenses matter for values only if their presuppositional objects exist and if the subjects for whom they are values exist, but in themselves they depend only on the thus-and-so of their presuppositional objects[6]. "It makes sense to attribute value to an objectum as a property, a capability to affect a subject regardless of what kind the subject is." It does not necessarily affect a subject, but under favorable conditions it may affect a subject and always in the same way, regardless of who the subject is. And there are apriori laws according to which values are interrelated[7].

Anything having impersonal value has value for any value subject and has also personal value, but not the reverse. There are many personal values which are not values for anyone else, as, for example, a photograph of my beloved pet which died some time ago has a value for me which it cannot have for any one else; or, to use Meinong's example[8], "A rich person values his treasure only under the condition that the treasure exists for him."

There are value errors. One can be wrong in attributing a value to an object, and one can also be right. This follows from the conception of absolute values and from the assumption that they can be known.

Since existence is not a prerequisite of absolute values, they depend on the being thus-and-so of their presuppositional objects. According to the nature of absolute values, they must be treated object theoretically, that is, apriori. Things of value which do not exist are e.g. the existence of a book, the story of a novel, a composition, the realization of a future plan. The value of the copy of an original painting lies in its similarity with the original painting, and this similarity does not exist, it is ideal.

---

[6] For the following see **Grundlegung,** pp. 135, 150.
[7] Comp. Chapter Seven.
[8] **Grundlegung,** p. 132.

Absolute values as ideal objects of higher order are eternally so. This is mentioned here because, for Meinong, absolute values are in an eternal state of being which Meinong called, then, subsistence. But, in this book "ideal" is used consistently instead of "subsistence," and the question of the length of their being becomes irrelevant. For if a value is absolute, it will be recognized as a value whenever someone thinks of it. Instead of speaking in ontological terms, I adopted the language of **...Gegenstandstheorie...** which speaks of theories, that is, languages. The Meinong of that work would use the term "ideal." (The very late Meinong and also the one of **Emotional Presentation** would say again "subsisting.") We have seen that values which seem to be strictly adherent to human conditions would have had to be there even before humans lived; they were then hypothetical and, thus, potential values. The problem is perhaps easier in respect to aesthetic values as e.g. beauty. Meinong, following Edith Landmann-Kalischer, had tried to see a parallel between the two following judgments "the sky is blue" and "the sky is beautiful[9]." The first judgment is a judgment of experience, the second judgment is apriori because beautiful is ideal and an object of higher order. However, even though the kinds of judgments are dissimilar, their evidence is immediate and their truth cannot be derived. The difference is that the first is a case of external perception and the second a case of internal perception[10]. Meinong calls the two judgments "irrecessive." They are basic and do not depend on other judgments. Beauty is not based on any human existence or subsistence, it is based on anything which can possibly be thought of to exist or subsist[11]. So beauty is a potential value as long as the object of beauty does not exist. The symphony in Beethoven's brain was just as beautiful as the one performed in a concert hall, perhaps even more beautiful.

Admittedly, Meinong's argument for absolute values is, all in all, very weak.

---

[9] This example is taken from **Em. Pres.**, 117; references to articles by Edith Landmann-Kalischer are to be found throughout.

[10] Compare Kalsi **Meinong's Theory of Knowledge**, chapter on internal perception.

[11] **Grundlegung**, p. 116.

It is interesting that values are not independent entities in the sense that individual objects are, but they need objects to which they can be attributed. If there are absolute values, they are independent of any subject's apprehending them or even inventing them. They hold universally as long as there are presuppositional objects for them, and even their presuppositional objects can be taken to be independent of place and time, they may be ideal.

In **On Emotional Presentation**, Meinong devotes a chapter to values in a more general sense. There he describes them and justifies his position concerning them through epistemological considerations which will be discussed in the next chapter. In the same book he writes on personal and impersonal (absolute) values. He defends his belief in absolute values in the following way: from the analysis of emotional presentation he turns his attention to its objects, namely to the values themselves without reference to their presentation. Traditionally, values have been considered from the standpoint of the valuing subject. That makes values appear and disappear with the subject and makes them dependent on the subject. If, however, the subject's valuation is merely the presentation of independent values, then values do not have to be presented in order to be. Also here the example of physics is brought in. As was stated above, physics is not dealing with phenomena but with that which produces phenomena. The same drive manifested in the physicist's research is, in general, manifested in the search for impersonal values. It is an empirical fact that some actions are seen as simply good or bad, without qualifications. Some objects of art or nature are simply beautiful, and there is no disagreement about it. And it seems that once a person's attention is called to these objects or actions there is no disagreement in their valuation. The easiest examples come from aesthetics. So, the awesomeness of a vast ocean, the beauty of a sunset, but even the goodness of St. Francis cannot and are not disputed.

Another argument is used in respect to the value beautiful which draws its strength from linguistic usage[12]. Grammatically speaking, "this is beautiful to me" is unusual, whereas "this is beautiful" is the accepted manner of speaking. The relativistic approach would have to

---

[12] **Em. Pres.,** p. 146.

be formulated as "I like this." Meinong does not claim this to be a convincing argument but as a fact that in certain realms of values the absolutist approach, at least linguistically, is more natural than the relativistic approach. The following approach is different: a fact which is known apriori is connected to concomitant real facts in which laws can be inductively detected, as e.g. counting in mathematics, collecting geometrical data and arriving by induction at properties of isosceles triangles[13]. Later Meinong suggests that a count of opinions could also inductively establish the universality of certain values, be they ethical or aesthetic. And so ends his argument for the apriori knowledge of absolute values and for the occurrence of absolute values. He expresses the hope that in later times a better solution may be found. Finally, in Chapter 8 his apriori method of relating value classes with each other is discussed. But it remains undecided if the classes themselves contain values which are absolute and are known apriori.

---

[13] **Em. Pres.,** p. 150.

Section 2

Chapter Five

Presentation of Values and Their Evidence

In the following I refer to **On Emotional Presentation** where most of the theory of the presentation of values was developed[1]. Values are presented by emotions. Meinong calls this emotional presentation. Specifically, values such as moral, aesthetic, and so-called timological values are presented by feelings. Values occasion obligations to realize those values. Obligations are presented by desires. These obligations are called "desideratives" by the Meinong of **On Emotional Presentation**. This term is not used anymore in **Elements of Ethics.** In that book Meinong speaks of values and valuations and then of obligations. There are three value classes: moral (or rather ethical which contains the moral value class as a subclass), aesthetic, and timological values. Timological values are truth and probability.

The question is: can emotional experiences lay the claim on being knowledge, or do emotional experiences have evidence, or at least an evidence analogy[2]? Evidence is a feeling of justification which accompanies judgments. It ranges from very weak presumptive

---

[1] **On Emotional Presentation**, Chapter 12; and also translator's Introduction.

[2] For the following comp. **M's Th. of K.** evidence chapter and references therein.

evidence to certainty. The degrees of evidence are not a part of objectives
or statements but are a part of psychic experiences of the judging person,
specifically of judgments. Evidence is indicated by a feeling of justification which accompanies the judgment when it occurs. Some
objectives are such that they can be judged with evidence by anyone.
This does not mean that, in fact, they are thus judged. A simple example
is that of any elementary arithmetic equation. Certainty as the highest
degree of evidence can only occur with certain apriori judgments. All
judgments of experience have merely presumptive evidence, some
empirical judgments approach evidence with certainty extremely
closely without completely reaching it. They do not reach it because they
are judgments of experience even though one cannot be mistaken in
many of them. For example, I know that I have a toothache when I have
it, and no one can persuade me that I am mistaken. But the fact that this
awareness is of an experiential kind instead of apriori knowledge
deprives it, for Meinong, of being capable of certainty. (This is not the
place to dispute his standpoint.)

It was stated that evidence is with judgments. It is not an
accompaniment of ideas. Feelings are analogous to ideas, desires are
analogous to judgments. Can desires themselves be evident? Meinong
discusses this question – which is a very difficult one within his theory
of knowledge – in **On Emotional Presentation**, chapters twelve and
thirteen. Desires which present obligations do not have any evidence.
They have a certain objective justification, not to be confused with the
feeling of justification. Their justification depends on the evidence of
value judgments[3]. That is, a value judgment attributes a value to an
object, action, or disposition. The corresponding desire presents the
obligation that this value be realized. Judgments concerning the value
of an object or an action or an attitude are not empirical because their
objects, namely the values, are ideal. The question is whether these
judgments are decidable at all. Meinong admits that, according to the
particular stage in his research, they are not; but he believes that they are
apriori (simply by the fact that their objects are ideal) and that
eventually a decision procedure can be found by which their evidence

---

3   Comp. **Em. Pres.** LXIV ff.

can be evaluated. Their evidence should be evidence with certainty because they are apriori[4].

As has been said, judgments have evidence. Desires are not judgments. They present obligations. But what about objectives which are about values, as e.g. the deed of a saint has the impersonal value good? According to Meinong, there are valuations which carry their legitimacy within themselves. He gives the following examples: "justice, gratitude benevolence carry the guaranty of their worth in themselves[5]." However mediated justification in valuations is often easier to see. This is analogous to mediated evidence in judgments, especially in judgments derived from premises. A form of mediated valuation is this: If B is valued with justification and A is its condition, then A is also valued with justification; or I am justified to value A. It is apriori certain that if I am happy about the existence or non-existence of an object, then I cannot, at the same time, be unhappy about it. In the same way, if I feel sorrow about the existence or non-existence of an object, I cannot feel happy about its existence or non-existence in the same respect at the same time. However, pleasure in existence does not always imply sorrow in non-existence. Meinong gives the example of an unexpected gift. If it had not been given, I would feel no sorrow over its absence.

Still, counter feelings, such as pleasure or gladness and sorrow, are part of the laws of valuation. These are not laws of how one actually does value an object, but laws of proper valuation. As was just said, they do not hold without reservations. If, however, someone is justified to feel pleasure in an object's existence, then he is justified to feel sorrow because of the object's non-existence. So, the justification of the valuations, not the actual valuations, are value-theoretically related. This is analogous to judgments which cannot (or one should rather say ought not) be thought without the ingredient of justification. These kinds of laws are recognized apriori[6], so they are a part of object theory[7]. That is,

---

[4] This was discussed in Chapter Four.
[5] For this and the following **Em. Pres**, Chapter 11.
[6] It was not until **Elements...** that Meinong made his theory explicit. See Chapter Seven below.
[7] Ibid. Chapter 11. This chapter is very important for the epistemology of valuations.

judgments about the laws of correct valuation are as evident as are the rules of deduction or simple tautologies. The justification indicates the presence of evidence.

A similar consideration concerns desires. The discussion is not focused on the fact of actually desiring something, because that is a matter of personal sensitivity, but the focus is on the justification of desiring, that is, of correct desiring. As there are rules of deduction, so there are rules of correct desiring[8]. Because of their presentative function, emotions are knowledge and take part in knowledge justification. "Justification" is to be understood as given by the feeling of justification accompanying presenting emotions. First, the analogy between feelings and ideas is considered: ideas are neither true nor false, but they may be called correct or incorrect if, on their basis, one makes a true or false judgment. If a feeling or desire takes the place of an idea, then the consequent value judgment may be justified or unjustified. The laws of value and desire mediation are not laws of factual valuation and desiring, they concern the natural togetherness of values and their presentation, regardless of what the subject does with them[9].

Feelings and desires are never judged to be justified if taken by themselves but always in relation to an object which is the presuppositional object of the feeling or desire in question. Analogously it is never correct or incorrect to have the idea "light"; in connection with aluminum it is correct, in connection with lead incorrect. If, then, an idea is correct if the judgment whose predicate stands for the idea is true, then a feeling may be called justified which presents an object (value) which is the predicate of a true judgment whose subject is the presuppositional object for the feeling (presenting the value). A presuppositional object for a feeling is any object which has a value as property and which is the occasion of a value feeling[10]. Emotional objects do not fulfill the conditions which objects of sense perception must fulfill. Beautiful is closer related to similar than to, say, blue. Similarity and beauty neither exist nor are externally perceived. Beauty at most can subsist or, as we would say, is ideal and, thus, belongs to apriori knowledge.

---

8   For the following **Em. Pres**, Chapter 12.
9   **Em. Pres.**, Chapter 12, p.118.
10 Reference to Edith Landmann-Kalischer, **Em. Pres.**, p.115.

Meinong turns his attention to desires which are associated with true judgments[11]. Judgments carry with them feelings called "judgment act feelings." The feelings vary with truth and degree of probability. Truth and probability are properties of judgments. The feelings are feelings of evidence here. Meinong speaks of truth feelings whose presuppositional object is the objective. It is noteworthy that Meinong connects these feelings with truth and not with falsehood. The connection between feeling and presuppositional object is necessary and can be seen apriori. In fact, it can be said that truth can be felt. Concepts of truth and experience of truth are related. Truth is a value whose presuppositional object is an objective, and truth is the proper object of the feeling of value. These are apriori insights into true judgments whose material contains emotionally presented objects. The task is now to find evident judgments whose predicates present emotional proper objects, that is, values. Prospects of accomplishing the task are admittedly not too good. At the time when Meinong wrote **On Emotional Presentation**, it was not possible for him to name a case where a value is attributed to an object with the same evidence as truth can be attributed to a factual objective. The only exceptions for him are extremely high moral values: love, justice, truthfulness.

In mechanics, for example, empirical knowledge must do where apriori knowledge cannot be achieved. That is natural because mechanics is dealing with reality[12]. But values are ideal objects of higher order, that is, they are based on their presuppositional objects. For there to be a value there has to be an object which has value. What could experience yield? The belief of one person is not particularly persuasive for another person, so says Meinong, and it is truly a very weak argument. The communal beliefs of a group is already a different matter. At last Meinong takes the following as a point of departure: if A is the presuppositional object for the value feeling p, whose proper object (value) is P, then the togetherness of A and P is reason for the assumption that A has P[13]. This is presumptive evidence and analogous to the evidence of

---

11   For the following Ibid., p. 117f.
12   Ibid, p. 120.
13   For the following Ibid, p. 121f. Compare with "Über die Erfahrungs-grundlagenunseres Wissesns" and **Meinong's Theory of Knowledge** with text references.

external perception. The presumptive evidence, however, does not concern existence but subsistence, that is, ideality. This evidence lies in the nature of the objects which are, properly speaking, subjects of apriori knowledge. In summary, it is not utterly impossible to know whether a given object has a value or not. So far, the approach to that solution is barricaded. But there is at least legitimate presumptive evidence.

Induction also has a role in the presentation of values. Meinong begins with an example from geometry. It is an ideal fact, known apriori, that the angles at the basis of an isosceles triangle are equal. But that fact can first be known by induction from data given by many drawings of isosceles triangles. Historically it was probably known in that way. So also with values. Via personal values one develops the thought of the possibility of impersonal values. If an objectum A, or rather the idea of an objectum A, evokes the emotion presenting the value N, then one may suspect that A is, in fact, the foundation for the value N[14]. To make the fact of foundation clear, Meinong picks up the example of comparison and the production of the ideas equal and unequal[15]. However, the situation is not quite the same. The evidence in emotional presentation of values, that is, objects of higher order, is not the same as that of intellectual presentation of objects of higher order. That has already been made clear. The evidence is that of justified presumption, quite weak in fact, but not entirely absent. The presence of presumptive evidence is supported by a consensus of subjects and, thus, can be used as an inductive approach. We must also remember that Meinong takes into account the more or less ethical and aesthetic talent in different people. And I think it is an undisputed empirical fact that some people are ethically and also aesthetically more sensitive than others, and that there are moral and aesthetic talents as well as there are musical and mathematical talents.

What I have written here was intended by Meinong to apply to aesthetic objects and values, but it is to be considered in analogy to ethical values. So, the text applies to ethical values or, rather, to all values. The point is that values are objects of higher order whose presen-

---

14   The reader is reminded of the foundation of objects of higher order and idea production.
15   **Em. Pres.,** p. 150.

tation is founded on ideas presenting existing or ideal objecta. The presentation of values is by feelings, which are produced like ideas of objects of higher order. However, the production of emotional presentation, even though apriori, lacks the certainty of the produced intellectual presentations. The difference must lie in the presentations themselves, one being intellectual, the other being emotional.

As far as aesthetic values are concerned, we are dealing with a "foreboding apprehension of the eternally beautiful" and the trust that there are, in these respects, gifted talents. But also here, in virtue of the ideality of objects, we are restricted to the apriori.

All in all, emotions may be called justified if the judgments which connect the proper objects of the emotions with their presuppositional objects are justified[16]. And this does not yield much for value theory.

---

[16] Ibid., 117.

Section 2

Chapter Six

Values and Valuations

A. **Personal and Impersonal Values**

Before knowledge – if there is any – of absolute values can be discussed, one must give careful attention to the epistemology of relative or personal values. For these are accessible to experience. The following is taken from Chapter Thirteen, "Personal Value and Impersonal Value," of **On Emotional Presentation.** That an objectum A has the impersonal value N is, under favorable circumstances, derived from the fact that A has the personal value N. That means the A-idea evokes a feeling which presents the value N. This presentation, by induction, may lead to a starting point of the search for absolute values. If the emotional presentation and the accompanying value judgment has any evidence, then the value experience is an indication of an impersonal value. If emotional value experiences are related to values as intellectual experiences are related to objecta and facts, then the personal aspect of values almost disappears[1]. Evidence for certainty is absent. If it were there, doubt would not be possible. There is only presumptive evidence. Knowledge which has evidence for certainty is apriori and immediate. Even though any possible knowledge of values would be apriori because values are ideal, the subject matter of values is, in fact, elusive, and Meinong admits that much.

---

1   Comp. **Zur Grundlegung der allgemeinen Werttheorie**, Vol. III of **Gesamtausgabe**, p. 150.

One factor in establishing a value is the consensus of subjects. Of course, this is problematical insofar as the subjects may be members of one culture. But in theory that circle may be widened to include a larger group up to the totality of mankind. The reader can easily see that Meinong has no argument in his favor here.

As has been pointed out in previous chapters, an object which has value cannot be the cause of a value feeling because it often does not exist; and for causal relationships, existence of the cause is a prerequisite. So, the object to which a value is attached occasions in one way or the other the feeling which is parallel to idea production[2]. The experience which occasions a value feeling may be an idea, a sensation, a judgment, or an assumption; at any rate, an intellectual experience[3]. An indication of good is gladness, an indication of evil is sorrow. Gladness and sorrow give rise to value feelings, together with the presentation of that which occasions sorrow or gladness in me[4].

There are no valuations without a subject, of course. But, in respect to absolute values, in none of the subject's experiences the subject itself must be apprehended as connected with the value even though he may be aware of his own value judgment. That awareness has nothing to do with the value experience itself. If a certain something is a value for me and it ought to be a value for any other subject, then the attachment "for X, Y, Z" to the valuation "O has value" is redundant[5].

B.   Actual and Potential Values

The constitution and surroundings or position of the object which has value, in respect to the value subject, are important[6]. Meinong gives the example of the value of gold in California before it was known to be there. Potentially speaking it always had value, actually speaking it received its value after it had been discovered and became a personal value for the people participating in the gold rush or others wanting to

---

2   **Grundlegung**, p. 57.
3   Comp. Chapter One above.
4   **Grundlegung**, p. 95.
5   Ibid., pp. 115 f.
6   For the following see **Grundlegung**, pp. 136, 146, 150.

acquire the gold. Here, values can be divided into actual and potential (hypothetical) values. But this does not really make a difference to the concept of value even if it is considered to be relative to a subject. In summary, personal value of an object lies in its meaningfulness for the subject. Which of these values can, then, be determined as absolute? Of course, for all valuations as emotional experiences there must be a subject, but not all values need a value subject.

At first, in order to support the belief that there are absolute values and that they can be presented as absolute values, Meinong appeals "to a rather comprehensive collective subject" who attributes the value to the value object. On the other hand, it was established above that often there are valuable things of which the subject is not aware, that is, where the subject does not experience a valuation at all, as for example a child may not value school. Still, others who are not themselves the value subjects do attribute value to the value object school. This lack of valuation depends on the consequences of facts or opportunities of which a person may not be aware at the moment. On the other hand, says Meinong, there are cases where no one would argue that faithfulness in work and love are good and dishonesty and maliciousness are bad. These values do not need a subject.

If, in fact, the truth of the value judgment depends on the truth of the presuppositional intellectual judgment, then the personal aspect is untouched as far as truth and error in the presupposition is concerned[7]. Intellectual judgment is a judgment about empirically or apriori verifiable objectives. For example, if it is true that a school education furthers a child's development, then the value judgment that school education is valuable for children is true also. Meinong uses the example of a sugar pill. Value is attributed to it only if it is believed to have medicinal power. To believe that it has medicinal power is an intellectual error. Thus, the attribution of value to the sugar pill is in error also. He states the same of the divining rod. If, in fact, emotional value experiences are related to values as intellectual experiences are related to facts, then the personal aspect disappears. The valuation is either correct or not. That is, value judgments are either true or false in the same way as perceptual

---

7   **Grundlegung**, p.150.

judgments are true or false. So a value would not be constituted by the value experience just as a true objective remains true forever regardless of who apprehends it in whatever way.

Meinong goes on as follows: psychological presuppositions for valuations are considered. They are the intellectual presentation of an objectum and an objective. They are the psychological basis upon which the valuation arises. He gives the following example[8]: clothing protects from the cold. This gives rise to a valuation of the clothing. "A key opens the door to my house." This is a fact which is intellectually presented by a judgment. The corresponding objective of the key's opening the door to my house is the object presupposition to my consequent feeling of approval and valuation of the key. This is a psychological process analogous to idea production where the idea of an object of higher order is produced[9]. Here another kind of object of higher order, namely a value, is presented by a feeling and then by a valuation based on the presentation of the object which is valued. That object either exists or is ideal. If it exists there is an actual value; if it is ideal there is a potential or also hypothetical value.

There are, thus, value errors. The value of an objectum is not created by the value experience directed to that objectum. For in that case the value would be created by my valuation and there could not be an error. That is, values would be a matter of personal preference. This is precisely what Meinong does not have in mind. As support for his claim of impersonal values, he uses the examples already mentioned earlier, namely that there are values of which I am not or cannot be aware even though they are acknowledged by other and better informed people to be values.

C.   Existence and Values

It has been said on various occasions that an object does not have to exist in order to have value. In **Zur Grundlegung der allgemeinen Werttheorie**, Meinong writes at great length about actual and potential

---

[8]   **Grundlegung**, p.99.
[9]   On idea production compare **Meinong's Theory of Objects** and text references therein.

value[10]. It is not my intention to unfold this rather complicated notion, but I would like to mention that it concerns also the existence or non-existence of objects which may have value. In respect to as yet non-existing but possible objects, Meinong uses the example of a pendulum clock. It cannot go if it has no weights. But there is the possibility that both the object pendulum clock with weights and even just pendulum clock may work. The difference here is that one object has more properties than the other, or, in Meinong's words, that one object is more determined than the other. But that has no bearing on their possibility. Just clock will suffice. Of course, any clock can work only if it exists. The non-existing pendulum clock cannot work. But the idea of pendulum clock involves the idea of its possibility of working. As such it is a hypothetical or possible object which has a value. Its value is also a neutral value. Personal value and even neutral value are bound to the subject or subjects for which they are a value. But the subjects need not be aware of it in order for it to be a value for the subject. Pendulum clock and its value subjects may both be hypothetical. It still has a value which is a possible or hypothetical value.

Concerning the distinction between actual and potential values, Meinong has much more to say. There are values which need an existing object in order to arise. For some predications, existence is characteristic. There are predications which contain, besides the thus-and-so, essentially a being[11]. Meinong gives an example from the first world war, which does not seem to have a direct bearing on the subject matter: low thundering noises in Graz are heard which are caused by cannon fire at the Italian front. To be an effect is a matter of thus-and-so, Meinong states, meaning perhaps that the characteristics of an effect depend upon its cause. Be this as it may, the point is that the reality of the cannon shots is an integral part of the meaning of such a statement, namely that there are low thundering noises to be heard in Graz. How can that example be understood and be used for values? There has to be an existing cause for an effect to occur. Only if both cause and effect occur can we speak of an instantiated causal relationship. The rela-

---

10   Section IV, paragraph 1 pp. 123 -125.
11   **Grundlegung**, p. 127.

tionship arises with the related events. However, when the events have passed, the causal relationship between them still holds and is possible ideal. Before the events occurred the causal relationship was there as a possibility, but it was not actually instantiated.

So it is with values. The cannon shots and the noise in Graz are the presuppositional objects of a causal relationship. The value objectum is the presuppositional object for the value. For a value to be actual and not just potential, its presuppositional object must exist. Money which is not there has no value, but if it were there it would have value. Buying power is possessed by the person who has the money, not by the person dreaming of being rich. But that does not influence the possible buying power of money. It is only that the occurrence of the actual power is tied to the existence of the money. Meinong uses the example of Napoleon on St. Helena where he, in fact, lacked power. But the Napoleon who once crowned himself emperor did actually have power. That power is hypothetical for the Napoleon on St. Helena.

These examples are used to make a distinction between actual and potential values, where the occurrence of the value is tied to the occurrence of the objectum of which it is a value. However, the situation can be potentialized by hypothetical statements. That is, when the value object is merely ideal its value remains a possible or hypothetical value, but as it is not instantiated it is not an actual value. Meinong spends a great deal of time and effort making the various distinctions in his monograph **Zur Grundlegung der allgemeinen Werttheorie.**

Meinong makes another, final attempt to secure impersonal or absolute values. Impersonal values can be values of objects which do not exist or for which existence is irrelevant or inapplicable. He appeals to truth as the most accessible absolute value. It is also an object of higher order attributable to objectives and is a special value, a logical dignity or timological value. Meinong claims that no one will insist on the relativity of truth. As a concession to dissenters, Meinong admits that the value truth may be subdivided into personal and impersonal value, and so the analogy remains. Some truths matter to some people and some do not, and some truths are absolute values regardless if they are acknowledged by anyone at any time or not.

The value of truth of judgments is presented by knowledge feelings. Also probabilities of judgments have a degree of logical dignity and corresponding knowledge feelings. I am not speaking of the feeling of justification which accompanies a judgment and indicates its evidence. Evidence is not a timological value. For evidence is an emotional ingredient of experiences and is not generated by experiences. It is not a property of objectives[12]. The point is that, in the whole realm of values, the presentation of values is emotional. These presentations are feelings in the case of values, parallel to ideas in the case of objecta. They are valuations, that is value judgments, parallel to judgments of objectives. They are desires in the case of obligations which Meinong also calls "desideratives." And obligations are always obligations to realize what is of value.

Timological values like possibility and truth of objectives, regardless if they are known apriori or empirically, depend upon the makeup, the thus-and-so of their carriers alone and are independent of existence. Objectives never exist anyway, they are about events which may exist at some time or other. Events are objecta. The carrier of the value is the object which has a value[13]. Let us not forget that Meinong takes it for granted that faithfulness and truthfulness are indisputably absolute values.

This is all that can be said concerning absolute values. And, all in all, it does not amount to very much. Meinong was painfully aware of that.

---

[12]   Compare **Meinong's Theory of Knowledge**, Evidence chapter and text references therein.

[13]   **Grundlegung**, p. 124.

Section 2

Chapter Seven

The Law of Omission, the Double Series of Potiores, and Related Problems

A. Introductory Remarks

In the beginning of the fragment **Elements of Ethics**, Meinong establishes the character of egoism and altruism. This is done basically by an empirical method, first inductively, by stating what people do or what attitude they show when they are called egoistical or altruistic. Then the purely empirical method is left behind and conditions are stated which must be satisfied by a person in order to be classified as either egoistical or altruistic. This procedure follows common usage of the terms as closely as possible. It goes deeper, however, insofar as it establishes a clear theoretical use of the terms. This procedure is not yet object theoretical even though it has apriori elements. It deals with what is given in the actual world in which we live. In the analysis of the following laws, however, the various relationships between terms which allow of gradations which have contraries and contradictories which, thus, establish classes of values or possibilities are not empirical anymore. There, Meinong is working within his object theory. In other words, this is apriori value theory.

B.   The Law of Omission[1]

Meinong tries to establish logical relationships between various ethical concepts. His interest focuses on implications and contradictions according to the Aristotelean square of opposites[2]. It is important to realize that the square of opposites is the matrix into which the concepts of value classes had to fit. It is also important to keep in mind that the first approach was the formulation of contraries. From the denial of contraries, other value classes were found. For example, Meinong began with the notion of the meritorious, which is the extreme end of the spectrum of moral values. The other end of the spectrum is the reprehensible. By negation of each of these two contraries, the other classes are found. Namely, by negation of the meritorious the permissible is found; by negation of the reprehensible the correct (or required, as Chisholm translates the term) is found. I will not engage in discussing the correctness of Meinong's procedure; Chisholm has done that. However, it must be emphasized that the term "permissible" designates a value class and does not designate the indifferent which is outside of any value class. The morally indifferent is no value and is represented, on the value line, by zero[3].

It is the relationship between these terms which underlies all subsequent analyses of other terms. Even though the value classes are ordered according to the traditional square of opposites, A, I, O, E, there is no implication from A to I or from E to O, that is, there is not an implication between the praiseworthy and the correct. That is, the Aristotelean implications from A to I and from E to O do not hold for the value classes. This is important to remember in connection with the same ordering of possibilities where such implications do hold and where there is one aspect where, as we shall see, the analogy between value classes and possibilities breaks down. The investigation of such analogies was very important for Meinong. Unfortunately, his comparison between value classes, modalities, and analogous series is

---

1   For comparison I refer the reader to **Deontic Logic: Introductory and Systematic Readings**. Ed. Risto Hilpinen, D. Reidel Publ. Co., Dordrecht-Holland, 1971.
2   This had already been pointed out by Chisholm in his **Ratio** article.
3   The value line will appear above.

incredibly complicated and, at places, murky at best. I shall attempt to make it as clear as possible.

If the terms are ordered in a linear series starting from the praiseworthy on the left proceeding via the correct to the morally indifferent (zero), and from the morally indifferent to the permissible and ending with the reprehensible, then there is a descending order from the praiseworthy over the correct to the morally indifferent, and, in the reverse order, from the reprehensible via the permissible to the morally indifferent. The ordering of the terms along a line is interesting insofar as it is the form in which Meinong investigates the relationship between moral terms and modal terms. The terms or the objects referred to by these terms are not points but are linear. There are, if you wish, infinitely many degrees of them. This at least is what Meinong stated in the earlier **Psychologisch-ethische Untersuchungen zur Werttheorie** and in the tenth chapter of **Elements of Ethics.**

The Law of Omission was first established in the commission and omission of acts which are meritorious, correct, permissible, reprehensible[4]. That is, the omission of a meritorious act implies that the omitted act is permissible (not excusable or indifferent). Meinong formulates the law thus[5]: "In general the following holds: the omission of a correct act is always reprehensible. This can be turned around: if someone could commit a crime but omits its commission, then his behavior is nothing but correct. It may be stated thus: the correct is correlated with a value domain on the other side of the value zero point in such a way that if a commission of an act belongs to one domain then its omission belongs to the other domain. In this way the correct is paired with the reprehensible. The law which connects both values is the Law of Omission." Further down on the next page: "The omission of the meritorious is permissible. It is easily seen that the reverse is also the case[6]."

---

4   Chisholm writes "required" instead of "correct" in **Ratio.** I shall keep "correct" as in "this is the correct thing to do" which, to me, captures well what is meant in German by "korrekt." Chisholm writes "excusable"; I prefer "permissible" here for the same reason.

5   **Psy.-eth. Unt.** p. 89.

6   This is the text which Chisholm justly criticized in his article "Supererogation and Offense: A Conceptual Scheme for Ethics," **Ratio V**, 1963.

These are called by Meinong "value classes." If a meritorious act is omitted, then the omission is permissible (not indifferent). Vice versa, if a permissible act is omitted, then the omission is meritorious. If a correct act is omitted, then the omission is reprehensible; and if a reprehensible act is omitted, then its omission is correct. Meinong does not claim that, according to the square of opposites, the commission of the meritorious act implies that its commission is also correct. He does not claim that the commission of a reprehensible act implies that it is allowed. However, there are fleeting doubts if, in fact, the implication of contradictions according to the square of opposites holds. A little later in the text Meinong admits that the omission of a meritorious act may imply several acts of different moral value. Moreover, the omission of the omission of an act does not necessarily imply its commission, so the Law of Omission does not comply with double negation where "not not p" is equivalent to "p." For example the omission of the meritorious only may imply that the omitted act is permitted or even reprehensible[7]. But, in the end, what is left of the square is exactly what is left of the square in Boolean interpretation. So, even though one might consider that "not A" may imply E, that relationship is denied; what is left is simply the equivalences of "not A" with O and "not E" with I. However, these doubts are based on the confusion of logical implication with material implication as is apparent in the use of "may imply." This has happened repeatedly in the course of the history of deontic logic, as e.g. with Ernst Mally who is widely considered to be the first to establish a formalization of deontic concepts. But really it was Meinong who initiated so many schools of thought.

Meinong addresses the problems arising from accepting the four classes as the basic value classes later in **Elements of Ethics** via a detour of modalities and then via the concepts of moral obligation and permission. The bringing in of meritorious acts, namely those which are supererogatory, leads to great difficulties, as Chisholm showed. The omission of the permissible, says Chisholm, does not imply the meritorious, as Meinong claims. Examples show that this is right. Meinong's point of view is as follows: when someone gives up what is

---

7   **Elements** (German text), p. 35. The numbers of the German pages are indicated in the translation.

permitted to do or to get, it is like a sacrifice; and the result is a meritorious act or situation. This explains why the omission of a permissible act is meritorious whereas a meritorious act is not required or correct, and its omission is permitted. The examples of which he must have been thinking led him to that result.

A better approach is the consideration of what is commanded, permitted, not commanded, forbidden, or what Meinong discussed later in greater and much confusing detail as obligation-to-be, permission-to-be, permission-not-to-be, and obligation-not-to-be. Even though his own discussions are partially mutually contradictory, they present concepts which are logically manageable.

C. Comparison of Some Modal Relationships with The Law of Omission

Meinong considered some modal relationships and formulated what he called the "law of the potius" and the "law of complements[8]." The concepts considered are factuality-of-being *(Tatsächlichkeit)*, possibility-of-being, possibility-of-not-being, factuality-of-not-being *(Untatsächlichkeit)*. Right in the beginning of this chapter I must say that the interpretation of these concepts as given in German – together with later-given concepts of obligation *(Sollen),* allowed *(Dürfen)*, not allowed *(Nicht-Dürfen),* not obligated *(Nicht-Sollen)* – is made very difficult by the fact that Meinong does not make clear what it is that is denied, the possibility or the being, or the obligation, *Sollen,* or the being of what is an obligation, *Soll Sein.* There is, however, one lonely definition given by Meinong which can be used to construct the definitions of the rest of the terms. In cases of extreme lack of clarity such as these, there is no choice but to leave his text behind, to take the material which is offered, and to interpret it in a consistent way which may or may not be what Meinong intended. But it should at least make some sense. We must remember that the text remained incomplete and unrevised by Meinong. And other texts written by him are no help.

---

8   In **Über Möglichkeit und Wahrscheinlichkeit,** paragraph 16.

Anyhow, Meinong calls the modal series "the double line of potiores" (meaning a gradation from possibility-of-being to factuality, and, reversely, from possibility-of-not-being to infactuality). This is graphically represented in the following way. (It may be that factuality is the same as necessity.) At any rate, factuality is not a line segment but a limiting point. The same holds of infactuality. There are neither degrees of factuality nor infactuality which is common sense. So we have two lines which contain a very apparent inherent flaw. But it is the basic thought which counts.

Factuality	Possibility +	Infactuality
1	9/10 1/2 1/3 1/4...1/9	0

Infactuality	Possibility -	Factuality
0	1/10 1/2 2/3 3/4...9/10	1

Factuality-of-being has the value 1, possibility-of-being, P+, is expressed in ratios, let us say, beginning with 9/10 to 1/2 to 1/9... with the limiting point 0, the point of infactuality. There are infinitely many degrees of possibility between the limiting points. Under the line, from right to left, factuality is 1 again, from there the possibility-of-not-being, P-, beginning with 9/10 and decreasing via 1/2 to 1/10.... The possibility lines work out fine, but the end points do not agree with the possibility series. They must be considered apart. If we want to express what I think Meinong had in mind, we must think of the possibility lines as superimposed upon each other and the T and UT points represented in the reversed order. The reason is that, at each cross section of the two lines, the two numbers of possibility must complement each other to make 1. If the upper line shows possibilities-of-being, the lower line shows the counter-possibilities which are possibilities-of-not-being. Meinong expresses them in the same way as possibilities-of-being, namely as positive fractions. Since they, together with the possibilities-of-being, are supposed to complement each other to make 1, they had to be written as was done above. The minus sign indicates how they are understood, namely, what is expressed as possibilities-of-being ought to be read as the reverse, possibilities-of-not-being. The difficulty with this graphic depiction arises when, from the UT point in the lower line, the possibilities-of-not-being should begin with a high ratio and decrease toward the T point. But it does not, and as it stands it does not make much sense. At any rate, Meinong formulates the following laws according to the graphical depiction of the "double line of potiores": To any given point on the upper line there corresponds a point on the lower line directly under it such that each possibility-of-being corresponds to a possibility-of-not-being. If the possibility-of-being is 1/3, its counter possibility is 2/3, etc., always resulting in 1. Factuality 1 corresponds to infactuality 0, both adding up to 1. This he calls the "law of complements." The possibilities at each cross section of the two lines which complement each other to make 1 are also called "coincidences," which, then, are named the "law of coincidences." It is, properly speaking, "the law of the coincidence of complementing possibilities." Furthermore, each point of a certain magnitude implies points of a smaller magnitude on the same line. Meinong calls this the "law of the potius." That is, if an objective has the possibility 1/2, then it also has the possibility 1/4, 1/5, etc. (Remember, this is not the case with the value classes.) So again factuality and infactuality are points or limits on the lines; possibilities are line segments, divisible into infinitely many points. Each point on the upper line coincides with a point on the lower line, and vice versa. The law of the potius holds for many other cases, by no means for all: Whoever is capable of lifting a heavy weight or playing a difficult piece of music is also capable of lifting a lighter weight and of playing an easier piece of music[9]. But whoever commits a meritorious act does not necessarily also commit what is correct or required. Law of the potius is good as long as zero is not reached. The law of complements presupposes that for each objective of a certain possibility there is only one complement, even though it may imply (not in the logical sense) infinitely many lower possibilities.

According to Meinong, one can depict the double line stretched out into one line beginning with[10] :

---

9   **Mögl.**, pp. 96-99.
10 **Elements** (German text), p.37.

Factuality	Possibility - of-Being	0	Possibility - of-Not-Being	Infactuality
I	II		III	IV

Expressed numerically it should look like this (Meinong does not write it out):

Factuality	Possibility - of-Being	0	Possibility - of-Not-Being	Infactuality
1	9/10...1/2...4/10...1/10		1/10...1/2...6/10...9/10...	1

But Meinong states this[11]: The features of the line are as follows. I, factuality is a limit, a point. II is a line consisting of infinitely many degrees of possibilities-of-being tending toward zero in the middle. On the right-hand side of the zero beginning closely to the point of infactuality, the line of possibility-of-not-being begins having a value approaching 1 and diminishing toward the limit of 0 in the middle. Then, so says Meinong, if I is denied we get any deliberate value within III, that is, the whole segment comprised under III. When IV is denied we get any deliberate values in II. If, on the other hand, III is denied we get I. Meinong does not explain clearly how that can be. But it can be made clear. The possibilities-of-being and not-being respectively can be thought as a disjunction of all possibilities. Then, when the whole disjunction III is denied, each possibility of that line segment is denied, and by the law of contradiction we get I. The same holds for the other side of possibilities-of-being; if the whole disjunction II is denied we get IV. If only one isolated possibility-of-being or not-being is denied, nothing follows by the law of contradiction. If points I or IV is denied, the result has to be the denial of the whole disjunction II or III.

The question is now how this law of contradiction, which holds for the so-called series of potiores (possibilities), compares with the actual square of contradiction, All S is P (A), some S is P (I), some S is not P (O), and no S is P (E). Meinong expresses his thoughts thus[12]: A is

---

11 **Elements** (German text), p. 37.
12 **Elements** (German text), p. 40.

a limit which has no more or less, it is a point. The same holds for E. I is considered as beginning with one S which is P, then increasing with many S's which are P limiting at all S is P, A. So, also in this interpretation, there is a limiting point and a series or disjunction of I's. The same holds for the other side of the square. E is the limiting point, all S is not P, or rather no S is P, for the series or disjunction of some S is not P, beginning also with one S is not P to many S's are not P. The result of denying A, I, O, E is the same as for the possibilities. Not-A implies the whole disjunction O; the denial of the whole disjunction O implies A. The denial of E implies the whole disjunction of I and the denial of the whole disjunction of I implies E. In this interpretation of the square, the analogy between the square of oppositions and the series of potiores is complete.

If one member of the I is picked as true, then all the "smaller" I's hold, too. For example, if seven S's are not P, then also six, five, four S's are not P. This is analogous to the possibilities where any point within the possibility line implies any point of smaller magnitude. Meinong actually confuses the issue by considering that when factuality is not the case, then anything within O and E may be the case. Also here he neglects the difference between logical implication and the material implication. But eventually he disregards this alternative and restricts his considerations to the contradictory relationships as explained in the previous paragraph.

The next question is if these relationships holding between factuality, possibility-of-being, possibility-of-not-being, and infactuality also hold between the members of the value line. Meinong approaches the subject matter by examining various examples. The first requirement is that the examples can be represented as a group of four concepts or value classes[13]. The next requirement is that the outer terms of the line must be point limits of lines which begin closely at zero and proceed toward their respective limits. The first example is that of certainty, justified certainty in the sense of evidence[14]. Certainty is the limit of justified presumptive evidence for an objective, certainty of the

---

[13]   **Elements** (German text), p. 39f.
[14]   Compare Kalsi **Meinong's Th. of Kn.** chapter on Evidence with text references.

negated objective is the limit of justified presumptive evidence for the
negated objective. The requirements are fulfilled.

D.   Moral Concepts and
the Law of Omission

Meinong goes on to discuss obligation and permission[15]. He
uses an example which in its original form remains incomprehensible
to me, but which seems to me to be repairable. The reason for the confusion lies perhaps in the German language and also in Meinong's own
formal notation. The terms considered are *Sollen, Dürfen, Nicht-
Sollen, Nicht-Dürfen*. According to the stipulations which Meinong
makes in the beginning of the chapter, the terms can be understood to
mean in English: obligation-to-be, allowed-to-be, allowed-not-to-be,
obligation-not-to-be. Obligations designated by "O" and allowed
designated by "D." Further he stipulates that the denial of the obligation
and the allowed be indicated by a "–" sign on the left-hand side of the
letters, and that the negation of being (namely that which is allowed or
obligated-to-be) be indicated by a "–" sign on the right-hand side of the
letters. According to Meinong the positive character of obligation and
allowed and of-being need not be indicated but ought to be thought by a
"+" sign. I prefer to write out all signs, for clarity's sake. Then
obligation-to-be becomes +O+, and obligation-not-to-be becomes +O-.
Allowed-to-be is +D+, not-allowed-to-be is -D+, allowed-not-to-be is +D-,
and not-allowed-not-to-be is -D-. For various reasons, among which is
the desire for greater precision, allowed-to-be is presented by the denial
of obligation. As I mentioned above, the only reasonable start can be
made with Meinong's one and only definition which is given at last on
page 49 of **Building Blocks of Ethics** (German text): allowed-to-be, +D+ is
by definition "-O-." With this in mind and only with this in mind, the
vocabulary can be established. Meinong's own account becomes confusing.

---

15   It is discussed in Chapter 13 of **Elements** (German text), p. 41ff.

1. +D+ = -O-

2. +D- = -O+

3. -D+ = +O-

4. -D- = +O+

Numbers 4 and 3 are contraries, and the reader may remember that Meinong begins his analysis with the establishment of contrary terms.

For reasons not clear to me, Meinong maintains that obligation allows gradations but permission does not[16]. Of course, that does not make much sense because D and O are related by equality. But if we let that stand, it is clear that the advantage of expressing everything in terms of obligation lies in the fact that then we are dealing with gradations in all four terms. Thus, they conform to the terms of the Law of Omission which are also capable of gradation. If the terms of obligation are ordered according to the square of opposites, the two contraries are at the top.

I	IV
+O+	+O-
II	III
-O-	-O+

The denial of I – that is, the denial of the left-hand side – implies III and vice versa, the denial of II implies IV and vice versa. Each member of the square is a disjunction of degrees of obligation. This situation was partially the case with modalities, and it works. Here again the conformity with the Law of Omission is shown. The conformity with the modal terms holds when they are represented in the square of opposition. The implication from I to II and from IV to III does not hold. However, I and IV are not limiting points but are capable of gradations, that is, all four classes by themselves are disjunctions.

---

16   **Elements** (German text), p. 41.

E.   Some Peculiar Consequences

Now, let us see to which other conclusion Meinong arrives. Let the following be the case (0 is the point of indifference):

+O+	+D+/+D-	+O-
...9/10...1/2...1/6...1/10...	0	...1/10...1/6...1/2...9/10...

+O-	+D+/+D-	+O+
...1/10...1/2...5 /6...9/10...	0	...9/10...5/6...1/2...1/10...

Written as double line following the example of the line of possibilities, with the same mistake in the second line, it looks as follows:

+O+	+D+	+O-
	...9/10...1/2...1/6...1/10...	

+O-	+D-	+O+
	...1/10...1/2...5/6...9/10...	

In this form it is seen that the series would complement each other if the D's were allowed to be lines and the O's were allowed to be points. But they do not make any sense with the understanding that the obligations are a series of decreasing value and not the D's.

So it turns out, quite as Meinong points out, that allowed is the zero point of degrees of obligation and that the series collapses into +O+...zero...+O-, where zero stands for -O+/-O-, and it is not a five, or rather four, member series anymore as in the examples above. This does not seem to be very consequential, but it must be remembered that every term is compared with the Law of Omission and the line of potiores together with their relationship to the square of opposites.

The representation given here does not follow the text exactly, the prefixes are different. But according to the definition given on page 49 of

Meinong's text, and taking it for granted that the contraries have to make the end points of the line, it consistently turns out to be quite right in Meinong's sense. It is also not indicated what value +O- would have; for if all that is right, according to the upper line, its limiting value should be 1. But then it would not be the complement of +O+, another reason why it does not make a double line of potiores.

The point is made that obligation admits of degrees but allowed does not. Why the latter is not the case I do not know, it is simply stated by Meinong that it is so. The result of this statement is that the obligation...allowed series does not agree with the modal line where the extremes of factuality and infactuality are points and the possibilities are lines. Moreover +D+ and +D- should be coinciding complements which they are not, according to the just mentioned statement, namely that they do not allow of degrees for whatever reason.

In the +O+ +O- line, simple negation does not follow the relationship of the four value classes because here we have only two members, obligation-to-be and obligation-not-to-be, which are contraries. But, according to my view, this series of two members is a distortion of the original series of obligations.

An example which does work, according to Meinong, is equality as limiting case of similarity and inequality as limiting case of dissimilarity. There, equality and dissimilarity are understood to be contraries and, thus, limiting points. They fit the double line of potiores and the square of opposites, of course[17].

Some cases fit the line of potiores, some cases do not, but all of these fit the square of opposites. The ones that do not fit the double line of potiores still fit the Law of Omission where all terms are classes of disjunctions. The Law of Omission applies to one series of potiores but not to the double series of complementing coincidences. Some series do not fit the Law of Omission because the end members are limiting points and not lines[18]. The reader is referred to the other examples in the translation included in this book.

---

[17]   For more examples see **Elements** (German text), p. 46ff.
[18]   **Elements** (German text), p. 51 and 49.

F.   Polar Opposites

Concerning the logical relationships between moral concepts perhaps the notion of polar opposites deserves to be mentioned. It is really quite simple. If we take two terms which are contraries in such a way that they are contraries only with each other, not with anything else, and if they allow a decrease toward zero from their opposite ends, then they are polar opposites. Even the corresponding points on the two segments proceeding from the zero point of indifference in the middle to their respective limits are, in a sense, opposites of each other. Examples of such polar opposites: right - left, top - bottom, equality - dissimilarity, great value - negative value (*Unwert*). It is to be noted that the line segments are incompletely determined objects which can be made complete or precise by definition of their various points or in terms of their limits and by negation as we have seen in the case of obligation[19].

But consider this: a line segment consisting of infinitely many or at least very many points is as such an incompletely determined object. The D's with the pre- and post-fixes were points and thus completely determined. When they were expressed as O's with varying pre- and post-fixes, they became line segments and, thus, incompletely determined objects. This was discussed in the chapter on incompletely determined objects above. However, it has already been established that the whole concept of incompleteness has its difficulties.

Meinong proposes the hypothesis that all polar opposites form a double series of potiores[20]. They are analogous to the Law of Omission (in the sense that they are segments as represented by I, II, III, IV ordered in a square analogous to the square of opposites) and follow the square of opposites.

The Law of Omission is a manifestation of two polar opposites, the meritorious and reprehensible, that is, very great value and negative value (*Unwert*) and their degrees converge at zero, the point of indifference, in the middle. But the negations I - III, II - IV remain[21]. Also I and IV are line segments. It must be a question of definition

---

19   See Chapter Three above.
20   **Elements** (German text), p. 48.
21   **Elements** (German text), p. 50.

where the borders between I, II, III, IV are. The remaining conclusions
are unclear.

Meinong is groping for the real difference between the Law of
Omission and other analogous cases, be they representable as double
lines of potiores or not. The text is quite obscure; the author states that he
is only conjecturing and refers to later thoughts which remained
unwritten. But some sort of sense can be made out of it, and the reader is
referred to the translation following this introduction for his or her
contemplation.

The main difference, so Meinong states at the end, between the
Law of Omission and its analogies is that the analogies deal with objectives of being thus-and-so. In other words, the objectives of the analogies
are all of the form S is P, where inclusion of S's in P may begin with one
S and limit at all S's. Even possibilities concern objectives of being
thus-and-so. (At this point I will leave aside the question as irrelevant,
whether all possibilities concern objectives of being thus-and-so or if
also objectives of being can be of a degree of possibility. Of course they
can! But let that be as it may.)

The Law of Omission deals with commission and omission of
volitions[22]. That is the being or not-being of volitions. The law concerns objectives of being. Meinong states, without giving a reason, that
the statement "If not: a certain volition is meritorious then that volition
is permissible" obviously does not hold. I fail to see what is so obvious.
So far, it has been accepted that the statements of the Law of Omission
had that form. But it seems that he means that if a volition is not meritorious it could be any of the other values - if the difference between the
two kinds of implication is ignored. That agrees with Chisholm's
assessment of Meinong's standpoint. Meinong tries to extricate himself
from this difficulty by stating that the Law of Omission deals exclusively with objectives of being. An explanation is not given. So we must
supply one. It may mean that if a meritorious volition is omitted then a
permissible volition is committed, even if there is no volition at all. If a
reprehensible omission is omitted then a correct volition is committed. I
am not sure at all if this saves the Law of Omission. What is saved is its

---

22   **Elements** (German text), p. 52.

distinctive difference from those analogous cases which follow the line
of potiores or even the double line of potiores. Meinong ends the chapter
by referring the reader to what had been written on page 32 of the manuscript concerning counter-feelings and counter-values (the reader may
look that up) and by stating that the Law of Omission deals with value
classes of the meritorious, etc., but not so much with the differentiation of
values as with the differentiation of obligations[23]. Death prevented him
from writing on that subject matter.

When this manuscript was published in 1968 in the third volume
of the Meinong **Gesamtausgabe**, an appendix was added which had been
written but not yet published by a student of Meinong and professor
emeritus of the University of Lublin, Franz Weber. He investigates the
relationships between the possibility of an objective and the obligation to
fulfill it. He constructs double series of obligations and compares them
with the double series of potiores. This shall merely be mentioned here.
The text is included in the following translation.

---

[23]   The manuscript pages are also indicated in the translation.

Section 2

Chapter Eight

Summary of Elements of Ethics

Part I, Chapter 1. It is noted that there are egoistic and altruistic values. But the ego is also the subject of altruistic valuation. There are values which are values for the subject and those which are not. Thus, value for the self has the ego as subject, and of course the ego is the subject of valuation. Value for the other has the alter as value subject. There is also impersonal value. Impersonal value in itself is a value for everybody. But what is neither value for the self nor value for the other is called neutrality value. Neutrality values amount to absolute or impersonal values. Meinong, by his overly subtle distinctions, makes the subject matter difficult to grasp, and one wishes to have Alexander's sword to cut through the convoluted and tight knot.

Chapter 2. A theoretical definition of the concept of egoism is given with reference to altruism: egoistical values are objects which stand in a special relationship to the ego. They lack an altruistic nature (the nature of altruism is not discussed, at this place); and if the ego is replaced by another subject, then the value ceases to be a value.

Chapter 3. It contains an empirical description of egoism. Tentatively, (p.11) all valuations have a subject who does the valuing. A value, valuation, or desire is egoistic if the ego is the only immediate subject in respect to the object of value in question. If the object stands in a "mine" relation to the ego in such a way that the ego cannot be replaced by another subject without canceling the ego as value subject, the singular position of the ego as immediate subject is guaranteed. According to Meinong, it is important to see if a valuation has several possible subjects or just one and if that one is the ego. This is a concept of egoism independent of the concept of altruism. The value subject is the subject for whom an object is of value. The value subject and the subject of the valuation do not have to be the same.

Chapter 4. Altruistic, neutral value, and the value position. Neutral value and neutrality value exclude ego and alter. In connection with the neutral value, the ego remains a value subject. In neutral values the ego is only one of the possible immediate subjects. Meinong uses the example of a threshing machine which is the communal property of several farmers. In egoistic, altruistic, and neutral values we have a differentiation of the position of the same value subject as immediate or remote. In egoism the ego is the immediate subject, in altruism it is the remote subject, and in respect to neutral values the ego is one of several possible subjects. For impersonal values no subject is needed. In the end, impersonal values are considered as morally significant. Meinong's remarks appended to the text are an important part of the text itself, and help to understand his intention better.

Chapter 5. There are two main classes of egoistical values: 1) some are experiences of the subject, accessible to internal perception and are relatively short-lasting (I know of my own experiences immediately by self-presentation and, of course, by memory); and 2) some are characteristics of the subject which are not accessible to internal perception because they are dispositions for experiences. Examples for the first group are a pleasant taste, a terrible odor; examples of the second group are health, sensitivity, intelligence. The first group includes psychic and physical experiences. Whatever affects the ego directly and is valued by the ego is egoistical value. Meinong spends several pages on clarifying these values. Any result which is obtained in the clarification is empirical. Meinong admits that so far he has not been able to give an apriori description which, for him, is the goal of any universal ethical theory.

Part II. Meinong discusses the objects of ethics and gives a characterization of ethics as theory.

Chapter 6. Ethics is dealing with value objects. Traditionally ethics was taken to be a practical discipline because it deals with values and not just descriptions of characteristics of objects. But now there is the goal of a general value theory which is theoretical and apriori. Logic is a part of the theory of objects and so is ethics. Value is the object of theoretical analysis.

Chapter 7. There are rational and empirical elements in ethics. Meinong discusses its method. Whether this or that object has value is at first an empirical question through recourse to actual valuation which does not prove that the object in fact has value. But the first step is empirical. Here, the Law of Omission is introduced for the first time. It is not, however, a generalization of what, in fact, people value. But from empirical data the moral philosopher arrives at general principles. He looks for laws describing the relationships between moral values. However, in actual valuations the egoistical and altruistic feelings of the valuing subject get into conflict with each other, and the altruism is measured against the egoism which has to be overcome. This is, for Meinong, an interesting fact, an object of empirical knowledge which has to be taken into account.

Part III. The Law of Omission is the center of attention. Since it has been thoroughly discussed in the preceding chapters, I will give just the briefest outline of the following chapters of **Elements of Ethics**. They are difficult to read, a great effort has to be put into interpretation of the rather obscure text.

Chapter 8. Omission of meritorious acts or volitions is permissible, omission of correct acts or volitions is reprehensible, and vice versa. Meinong believes that this is generally accepted. The law is empirically verified by actual valuations, non-empirically made more precise through differentiation and sharpening of concepts. *Überwert* (supererogation) and its position in regard to negative value *(Unterwert)* is discussed. The corresponding counter feelings of approval and disapproval are empirical so far, but are perhaps founded on a value law which may be known apriori.

Chapter 9. An object theoretical, that is, apriori interpretation of the Law of Omission and of the law of double negation is given. The

Law of Omission may be a special case of a more general law.   Its relationship with double negation is discussed.

Chapter 10.   Analogous cases of the Law of Omission are considered.   Meinong studies various groups of values which he tentatively considers to be analogous to the Law of Omission.   I refer, here, to Chapter 8 of this introduction.

Chapter 11.   Modal series of factuality, possibility-of-being, possibility-of-not-being, inactuality are studied and compared with the value classes.   Here I refer to the same Chapter 8.

Chapter 12.   The discussion of analogous cases is continued which are to be understood as double series of potiores, gradations of intensity or magnitude of various properties or actions in their analogy to modalities.   The double series of potiores is given in detail in **Über Möglichkeit und Wahrscheinlichkeit,** Chapter 16.   It is an ordering of modalities of being, on the one hand from factuality-of-being over possibilities-of-being to infactuality and, under it, an ordering of infactuality-of-being via possibility-of-not-being to factuality-of-being. This double series is quite problematical as the reader can see in Chapter 8 above.   Meinong sees a close relationship between uncertainty of knowing and possibility-of-being and of not-being.

Chapter 13.   Analogous cases of different kinds are considered.   I have not discussed each of these cases in the preceding chapters of my text.   The reader may do that for her/himself.   At closer look, some seeming analogies are not analogies, according to Meinong.   In some cases there are analogies of modal series and there are analogies of the value series.   If a series is analogous to one it is not analogous to the other for formal reasons.   See Chapter 7, Section 2 of this book for further details.

Chapter 14.   It is noted that analogous cases have general marks in common.   The notion of polar contrast is introduced.   It deals with contraries, which are exclusively contrary with each other and nothing else, and a series of diminishing terms on each side of the contrary pair where each term of the diminishing line of one contrary is paired with the corresponding term of the diminishing line of the other contrary.   I must again refer to Chapter 7, Section 2 of this book. For brevity will be of no use here.

Chapter 15. The Law of Omission is compared with its analogies. I refer the reader to Meinong's own text. Meinong attempts a solution of his theoretical difficulties by pointing out that factuality and possibility are attributed to objectives and are, thus, objectives of being thus-and-so. The Law of Omission deals with actions and omissions which are not objectives of being thus-and-so but are objectives of being. The explanation given seems a little contrived as the reader can see for her/himself. The upshot is that the Law of Omission is not analogous to many cases of seeming analogies from areas outside ethics.

Part IV, Chapters 16 and 17. The book ends with a logic of valuations. It refers to the older Text **Psychologisch-ethische Untersuchungen zur Werttheorie** which contains a description of how people actually value things. Now Meinong amends the earlier version by describing what should reasonably be valued according to apriori deliberation. He again refers to the various values – egoistical, altruist, neutral, and neutrality values – which were discussed in the beginning of the fragment. There seems to be a relationship between values and actual valuations which follows certain regular patterns. They are laws of valuations, still very empirical but perhaps accessible to apriori knowledge, as Meinong hopes. A graph was added to the text by Ernst Mally.

Section 3

Alexius Meinong:

Elements of Ethics

Professor Ernst Mally – Graz, who died in 1944, wrote the introduction
for the following text which was prepared by him for publication:

"The posthumous work remained incomplete. I have treated the
manuscript in the same way as I have treated **Zur Grundlegung der
allgemeinen Werttheorie**: nothing was changed except evident
mistakes. If possible I completed the literature references; loose notes
within the text were included in the appended additional notes. They are
referred to by numbers in brackets. The headings which I put into the
text are also indicated by brackets.

Graz
February 23, 1921"

Additions of the editor are in brackets followed by *.

Rudolf Kindinger
Editor of Volume 3
Gesamtausgabe

Section 3
Table of Contents

Section 3, Part I

Chapter One

Value for the Self, Value for the Other, Neutrality Value

[1] (Selbstwerte, Fremdwerte, und Neutralwerte)

(Ms. p. l.) 1. There are only a few ethical concepts which have been engraved upon popular, pre-scientific thinking. Among them are, for example, the contrast between egoism and altruism. One of these two terms achieved relative popularity whereas the other term remained for the most part the exclusive property of theoretical thought. Thus, it seems that only one of these terms was thoroughly studied. And this is not merely true of everyday life but also of the trend of theoretical thinking. It is peculiar that the relatively complete concept belongs to the less popularized term, and that the incomplete concept is joined with the popular term. It is the task of our theoretical investigation to concentrate our efforts on concepts which have not been fully developed. For years I have been working on a solution[1] of the problem. In the meantime, important questions will be raised again; and I hope that I will be able to help obtain a clearer insight into a situation which appears occasionally to be quite convoluted.

---

[1] In **Psychologisch-ethische Untersuchungen zur Werttheorie**, Graz, 1894, pp. 95 ff.

First of all, it is surely superfluous to point out that the adjectives "egoistic" and "altruistic" do not merely refer to desires – as I myself once believed – but that they refer also to valuations and finally to values[2]. When one speaks of egoistic and altruistic values, it is primarily suggested that one should ascribe meanings to these expressions / (p. 2) which they really do not have but which are sufficiently important and useful to be retained. However, special terms should be assigned to those meanings. Etymologically speaking it could already have been established that a value is egoistic if the ego is the subject, altruistic if the alter is the subject. However, that this is not so can be seen in the fact that I myself have altruistic desires and valuations besides egoistic desires and valuations. Thus, no objection should be raised against the possibility that there are altruistic and egoistic values for me. Then, the ego is the subject even of altruistic values. But the altruistic nature of those values must be grounded on something other than the value subject.

In the following, it will be discussed what that ground may be. At first it might be recommended to study other terms which belong by nature to the subject – as is the usual practice in value studies; the meanings of these terms must still be precisely determined. We must be careful that the reference to the subject is not taken to be made to an individual subject or a concretely determined subject but that it is a reference to individuals in general. A certain universality of thought and, consequently, of expression can be achieved only if the subject referred to is apprehended by a relative determination, that is by making the subject identical with the speaking or thinking subject in question. In the second case the value and its objectum, namely the good or the bad, are "extraneous" to the subject. In the first case, the value and its objectum are the subject's own. Thus, in respect to the latter, one can speak of value in itself (*Eigenwerte*) or good in itself. In the former case one can speak of values for the other and goods for the other (or extraneous values and goods). In fact, once[3] I used these expressions occasionally in the proposed sense, and other authors followed my usage.

---

2   Ibid,. p. 95 et al.
3   Compare **Psychologisch-ethische Untersuchungen...**, p. 112.

I had pointed out that the term "value in itself" (*Eigenwerte*) assumed a double meaning after it was set opposite to "derived value" (*Wirkungswert*) by Christian v. Ehrenfels. But I did not sufficiently emphasize my objection to the questionable and ambiguous meaning, I did not want to give up the otherwise natural way of expression.

However, my long experience with the use of language proved me wrong. The concept of value in itself in the sense used by v. Ehrenfels has a much too fundamental meaning to open it to an equivocation by introducing a secondary meaning / (p.3) even if the secondary meaning is made understandable and acceptable beside the fundamental meaning. Thus, we need a new expression here. Without being too arbitrary I think I may propose the expression "value for the self" (*Selbstwert)*, and in analogy to that the expression "good for the self" and so forth. Its counterpart "value for the other" (*Fremdwerte)* is still unobjectionable. In summary we can give the following definition: value for the self is the value whose subject is the ego, value for the other is the value whose subject is the alter, the other person.

H. Schwarz seems to have adopted the expression "value in itself" (*Eigenwerte)*[4] in the sense in which it was used in **Psychologisch-ethische Untersuchungen...** which we have given up. He uses the expression "value for the other" for all values which are not values for the self. Such a negative definition of "values for the other" can agree with my positive definition only if there were not any other values for the ego or for the alter. At first glance it could be agreed that these conditions should naturally in all cases be fulfilled. However, there is already at least one case where these conditions are not satisfied. I am thinking of the possibility of an impersonal value whose actual occurrence cannot be doubted. I gave the reason for my belief at another occasion[5]. A second exception is immediately recognized when one considers – as one well should – the ego and the alter not merely as subjects of value for the self and value for the other but exclusively as subjects of values for the self

---

4   Comp. H. Schwarz, **Das sittliche Leben**, Berlin, 1901, e.g. p. 215, et al.
5   Comp. my discussion of this matter in **Über emotionale Präsentation** in the proceedings of the Imperial Academy of Sciences in Vienna, philosophical-historical division, 1917, Vol. CLXXXIII and par. 13 [**Zur Grundlegung der allgemeinen Werttheorie**, Graz, 1923].

and values for the other. Under these conditions we find already, among personal values, such values which are neither exclusively values for the self nor values for the other because both the ego and the alter are the subjects. The just mentioned first case is always accompanied by the second case because if an object has impersonal value then it has also personal value for anyone who recognizes the impersonal value and who, consequently, values the object in question. This object, of course, has value neither just for the ego nor just for the alter. From the standpoint of both, it is neither value for the self nor value for the other. That which is neither value for the self nor value for the other will be called "neutrality value" *(Neutralwerte)*, / (p.4) in the following[6]. [2] Thus, value for the self, value for the other, and neutrality value constitute a complete disjunction in the realm of values.

---

6   "Neutrality value" and "neutral value" are not synonymous for me. More about this on Ms. pp. 6,15.

Section 3, Part I

Chapter Two

Egoism and Altruism,
a Stipulative Definition [3]

In the preceding chapter we were dealing with words and the determination of their meanings. Thoughts which naturally arise in this context did not require a strict determination. But now the clarification of thoughts concerning the meaning of the terms "egoistic" and "altruistic" is meeting with unexpected difficulties, at least as far as one of the terms is concerned. Naturally, the words indicate directly that ego and alter are opposites. As in all such cases, whenever ego or alter are spoken of, we are concerned with the point of view of the thinking or experiencing subject. But as even altruistic values, valuations, and desires are, first of all, values, valuations, and desires of the ego, the contrast between egoism and altruism does not concern the subject as has already been acknowledged. The contrast should concern the objective elements in the values, valuations, and desires in question. This becomes evident when altruism is considered. As has been said above, the theoretically naive person is as familiar with altruism as he is unfamiliar with the term "altruistic." Everyone knows that, under certain circumstances, he focuses his desire on the well-being or woe of someone other than himself. And when he becomes enlightened that such desire is called "altruistic," he is also well acquainted with the meaning of the word. Then it is only natural to explain the meaning of the word "egoistical" in an analogous fashion. And since everyone is his own best friend, as one likes to put it, it seems to come natural to assume that the concept of altruism is formed in a fashion parallel to the concept of the egoistical. Even though this seems to be the natural way of dealing with the matter, it gets one into unexpected difficulties. It is the most important task of our theoretical work to overcome these difficulties.

/ (p. 5) For the time being we can safely conclude that we are not dealing with phantom difficulties which are often, with great insistence, pointed out in connection with the concept of altruism. At this point the ancient question is raised again how my being interested in something which is expressed by way of valuations and desires can be the genuine interest for someone else's desires, or, better, someone else's experiences. In the beginning of my studies of value feelings, it became quite clear[1] that our valuations and, therefore, our desires can concern themselves with the experiences of others as well as with anything which is accessible to our apprehension and judgment. We could possibly ignore the objection that there are no altruistic valuations and desires because all valuations and desires are by nature egoistic[2]. This objection could be ignored because it concerns only altruism. However, the objection is rooted precisely in that theoretical attitude about egoism which must be studied at great detail here. Even though this theoretical attitude denies the possibility of altruism egoism can best be understood if studied in analogy to altruism. When it is recognized that the "well-being and woe of the alter" rests in the center of altruism, it can be stated more precisely that we are dealing with objecta which are also value objecta for the value subject "alter." Egoism can be characterized in the same way: one's own well-being and woe in general concern objecta as far as they are value objecta of the value subject "ego." Now, no ego, that is, plainly nobody, can value anything without being the subject of the valuation. This is only a tautology, but it is correct. In the same way, no ego can desire anything which is not a value objectum for him. Thus, all valuations and desires of the ego, that is, simply all valuations and desires, should be called egoistic as far as they have the characteristics

---

[1]   Comp. **Psychologisch-ethische Untersuchungen...**, pp. 42 ff.
[2]   Ibid., pp. 96 ff.

common to all egoism. From this it follows, however, that, in principle, the possibility of altruistic behavior must be denied.

The most striking characteristic of this point of view is that it begins with egoistic values and ends with values for the self *(Selbstwert)* as defined above. For a value / (p. 6) whose subject is the ego is a value for the self. Consequently, altruistic value should be a value for the other which, as has already been mentioned, is not possible. Apparently, there must be a mistake. The mistake is most likely uncovered by the fact that we, in characterizing egoism, found ourselves suddenly going back from the value object to the value subject. This mistake does not occur in connection with altruism. In egoism [4][3] [it is appropriate to reach back from the value objectum to the value subject, because the value objectum in the sense indicated here seems to be fully determined by this subject. This is not the case with altruism. There, the value objectum in question is not determined by the value subject (ego), but by the alter: the value objectum in altruism is given from the beginning with the "well being and woe" of the alter. Insofar, egoism and altruism would commonly be different from each other in this, that the proper value objectum is given with the ego in egoism but given with the alter in altruism.

But likewise art, science, culture are valued or desired; and our attitude in these cases is neither egoistic nor altruistic. Nevertheless, it should constitute a case of egoism, according to the definition above since there is no alter given with the value objectum. The so-called cultural goods, which are really meant here, concern the ego and the alter in equal measure. Values or desires of this kind I have called "neutral values" and "neutral desires[4]." However, in contrast with them I characterized egoistic values and desires by the positive determination that the objecta of egoism are connected with the ego by a special relation which I called the "relation of mine" *(Meinheitsrelation)*[5].]

---

[3] Leaf #10 is missing in the original manuscript. A supplement was suggested by Prof. em. Franz Weber, Ljubljana. It is translated and inserted into this text within brackets. The original is located in Meinong's literary remains, Karton XXX, in the Manuscript Collection at the University of Graz, Austria (the translator).

[4] **Psychologisch-ethische...** p. 103, 113 ff. I will return to the relationship between "neutral values" and "neutrality values" on Ms. p. 15.

[5] Ibid., p. 101 f.

Generally speaking, even today these determinations seem still to be useful. But the "relation of mine" appears so very general that it seems to extend far into the neutral domain. The painter calls his painting "his" art, the historian or anthropologist calls culture "his" work project. Every object is mine which stands in any sort of relationship to me. "My" forefather, "my" friend, "my" superior, "my" neighbor, "my" adversary, "my" shadow, "my" likeness, "my" opponent, "my" property, "my" danger. These are random examples for the vast manifold of that which can be called "mine." However, "mine" does not mean anything else but "that which is in some way related to me." But this characterization cannot be used to describe egoism in contrast to anything which falls into non-altruism. Still, this problem can be resolved. The condition that the objectum of an egoistic valuation or desire / (p. 7) must stand in some relationship to the ego is always satisfied and, therefore, trivial. If the ego is seen in such a light and if the valuations and desires of the ego would be replaced – all things being equal – by someone other than the ego then the difference between non-altruism and egoism becomes sufficiently clear. Thus, we get a somewhat peculiar but sufficiently clear relation between objectum and ego. In a very narrow sense of the word this relation is called "relation of mine" *(Meinheitsrelation)*. In summary, the following can be said, and I think no objections will be raised against it: values, valuations, and desires are called "egoistic" when they are not altruistic and when their objectum bears such a relationship to the ego that they disappear if the ego is replaced with another subject.

There seems to be no objection against this characterization of egoism. The relation between ego and objectum, which has just been made more precise, can be present and still there is room for a certain altruism. Take, for example, the interest of my friend which, in an important sense, is characterized by his relationship to me. I act altruistically and not egoistically when I look after his interests. I was considering this possibility when I first discussed these matters[6] while I was formulating the concept of the selfish – altruistic *(Selbstisch-Altruistische)*. The following situation, however, can provoke a doubt

---

6   **Psychologisch-ethische Untersuchungen...**, p. 103.

where a valuation or desire which clearly deals with the well-being or woe of another person can still maintain an egoistic character. When someone refuses to help a person in need because, as he might say, he is so sympathetic that he cannot bear the sight of the other's misery, we will without hesitation call this attitude egoistic on the ground of which something happens or rather fails to happen "out of sympathy." When we give presents to children with the direct purpose of receiving pleasure from their happiness about the gifts, then our action is not free of egoism. At closer look, there is nothing in this which contradicts our determinations given above. We are only dealing with circumstances which are unusually compound. The sympathy in one case and / (p.8) the being happy for someone in the other case are surely altruistic. Still, a valuation or desire which is directed toward the sympathy of the ego surely cannot deny its egoistic nature. Here, egoism and altruism are joined in a peculiar union. It depends upon several conditions if, in the total aspect of a situation, egoism or altruism dominates.

Section 3, Part I

Chapter Three

A Natural Definition of Egoism

Our description of egoism covers the relevant fact easily and freely. Still, a certain feeling of dissatisfaction remains as is always the case with artificial definitions. But, by the very fact that in everyday life the concept of egoism is so casually used, it is indeed desirable to look deeper into the nature of egoism in order to find a better definition. [5]

For our efforts in this direction it seems best, at first glance, to proceed again in analogy to altruism. The analogy concerns the object and not the subject of the attitude in question. The object of altruism is the well-being and woe of the alter, as we may say. This surely means that it is concerned with objecta which lie (really or supposedly) within the sphere of the alter's interest. Could egoism not simply be determined by replacing the word "alter" with "ego"? Then any valuation or desire would be called egoistic whenever it is concerned with an object which has a real or assumed value for the ego. And, in fact, we are familiar in everyday life with this thought in its simple and transparent form. There is no doubt that any attitude conforming to it will, without hesitation, be classified as egoistic by the general public. On the other hand, not everything which is called egoistic fits into this mold. So it is justified to ask if a correction of the notion should be made.

A first example is given by the desire of a hungry or thirsty person for food or drink. / (p. 9) This desire is surely egoistic although, in general, he will not think of the value of the desired object. He thinks that, in some way, the realization of his desire is connected with pleasure, and a fantasy feeling is combined with the assumption of the realization of the desire[1]. This is, of course, different from the case when something is desired expressly for the reason that it has value for the person who desires it. This touches upon a situation which falls out of the generally accepted parallelism between egoism and altruism. A similar objection was raised against the attempt to determine altruism from the viewpoint of the object. Concerning the "well-being and woe" of the alter, not only that is important which evokes a value feeling in him, but everything which causes in him pleasure or pain of whatever kind. In spite of this, the characterization of altruism as given above remains good. The reason for this is that whatever gives pleasure or pain can be subsumed under value or disvalue *(Unwerte)* so that the altruistic person can correctly subsume them under this disjunction. The egoist can do that, too. If egoism and altruism were characterized by that which one has a right to do, then both of them would have to be called egoistic whenever they are focused on an object which lies in the value domain of the ego in question. (It does not matter how subjective the value domain is.) With this we would have returned to the point of view from which all valuations and desires would pass for egoistic. Thus, the example of food and drink given above must be considered in the following fashion: in our desires, not only valuations but also other feelings of pleasure or displeasure are important which provide a kind of pleasure background "in view of which[2]" the motives for the relevant desires are given. According to this, any valuation and desire is egoistic whenever it aims at an objectum as a value or pleasure objectum for the ego.

In the meantime it has become apparent that this outline / (p. 10) of egoism is not wide enough. This may not seem believable to anyone for whom, according to widespread belief, it is a matter of course that all desires are really a craving for the object proper or at least for the motive. This misconception applies[3] to cases where a behavior is

---

[1]   Comp. **Ann. II**, p. 321.

[2]   "In view of which" must be understood somewhat technically. Compare **Ann. II**, p. 176, and **Mögl.**, p. 431 et al.

[3]   Compare also **Psychologisch-ethische...**, p.96 f.

egoistic without having the just described characteristics. Anyone desiring to be honored or valuing a received honor is egoistic. But where would the value feeling or other feelings of pleasure be which constitute egoism, according to what has just been related? Perhaps one feels inclined to answer that an ambitious person desires honor because he puts value in it, and indeed, his desire could easily be motivated by that. But what about the motivating valuation itself? Is it not egoistic? That is not so easy to say: for then the egoistic aspect of an attitude cannot be bound to a motivation by one's own value or other pleasure feeling. Without a doubt, the ambitious person is satisfied by an honor when he receives it. He may know this, and knowing it he may desire honor. But the satisfaction itself, although being egoistic, cannot be motivated by value or pleasure. For value, at least as far as it is personal value (impersonal value is out of the question here), is founded on this satisfaction as an experience of value. This satisfaction itself cannot be founded again on value. A value feeling which is founded on a value which itself again is founded on the value feeling is, value theoretically speaking, as impossible a thing as the old *causa sui*. As far as I can see, we failed here in our attempt to clarify the pre-theoretical concept of egoism in analogy to altruism.

We may get nearer to the goal by the following considerations. People working in the area of the theory of values or the theory of desires are quite familiar with the fact that valuations and desires are concerned with their objecta, partly directly, partly through the mediation of other objecta. The contrast between value in itself (*Eigenwerte)* and derived value (*Wirkungswerte*), which was touched upon above[4], illuminates this fact (it can be added to other cases of transfer values). / (p. 11) But I believe that, so far, one has neglected to take notice of the fact that transfer of this kind does not only occur with objecta but also with subjects. When the state of a sick person or a person involved in an accident evokes my sympathy, then I am, without a doubt, the subject of a valuation whose object is the other person's state. But usually such a state causes sorrow in me because it causes sorrow in the other person. I am justified to say that I am the value subject for the value

---

[4] Compare (p. 2 f) above.

object in question by way and through the mediation of the other person. We do not want to overuse the terms "mediation" and "transfer" by using them in a new and different sense, since they are normally used in connection with objecta. Thus the following could fittingly be said: The other person is the immediate subject, but I am the more remote subject of the valuation in our example. It can at once be seen that an analogous statement can be made in respect to desires. [6] The differentiation between immediate and remote subject opens up new possibilities for the characterization of egoism and altruism by special consideration of the immediate subject. This thought can be tested by calling a value, a valuation, or desire egoistic when the ego functions as the immediate subject. And values, valuations, and desires are called altruistic when the ego takes the position of the remote subject and the alter takes the position of the immediate subject. The advantage of this characterization is not only its simplicity but also the fact that egoism and altruism are treated in a parallel fashion. This has been suggested from the very beginning by pre-theoretical thinking which has been explored here.

Still, there seems to be a case where the new concept of egoism fails. A person interested in the arts endeavors to discover new talents. Something similar is true of supporters of the sciences or scientists themselves. Is such an endeavor altruistic? Or could it be said that someone who found his happiness or fortune in the arts or sciences wants other people to enjoy the same happiness or fortune? So many a person who learned how typical it is in many areas of human endeavor that capability and luck do not always go together continues to recruit new talents for the arts and sciences. He does not do so exclusively, or perhaps not at all, for the sake of someone else's welfare. He does not do it for the reason that the alter takes the position of the immediate / (p. 12) subject or at least the position of a more remote subject. The ego, then, is the immediate subject: still, his effort is not egoistic and is, without a question, neutral. Although there are many reasons in favor of utilizing the immediate subject for the characterization of egoism, it fails in the case of a neutral attitude.

It is immediately clear that the consideration of impersonal values, in this light, leads to the same results as the consideration of neutral values: The ego can focus on an impersonal value which has other subjects than himself. Still, the desires and valuations in question are not egoistic. Apparently the introduction of an immediate subject is not enough to characterize an attitude as egoism. The possibility of several immediate subjects must expressly be denied. The meaning of the expression "immediate" should indicate exclusiveness and singularity. But still one can say meaningfully that there are possibly two immediate and equally short routes from Point A to Point B, not counting various detours. In the interest of clarity the following expression is preferable: a value, valuation, or desire is egoistic if, in virtue of the nature of the objectum in question, only the ego can be the immediate subject. This is never the case with neutral or even impersonal value: it is always possible that there are several if not infinitely many immediate subjects. Thus, we are in the favorable position to be able to state that, in egoism, the very nature of the objectum does not admit a plurality of immediate subjects. The concept of "relation of mine" comes to mind, which was made precise above. It already proved itself to be useful in the characterization of egoism. The exclusiveness of the ego as immediate subject is guaranteed if the objectum is related to it in such a way that the ego cannot be replaced by another person without ceasing entirely to be the value subject.

If this is true, then the following question is raised: Is the attitude of egoism always connected with a singular immediate subject? When several farmers get together to buy a thrashing machine, each one of them is normally acting egoistically. Several immediate subjects show their interest, and basically, / (p. 13) any egoistic pooling agreement seems to be incompatible with the condition that there can be only one immediate subject, regardless if there are a few or many participants in the agreement. Here, something is felt which is obvious and a matter of course, but which is often overlooked because it is so obvious: we must ask if the value which I attribute to the means by which the goal is obtained is egoistic or altruistic. Apparently that depends upon the altruistic or egoistic character which the goal may have. Generally it can be said that the contrast between egoistic, altruistic, and neutral concerns values in themselves *(Eigenwerte)*. According to the quality of the values for the self, the transfer values are qualified which originate from the values for the self. In agreement with Christian v. Ehrenfels[5] they can suitably be called parent values (*Stammwerte*). Clearly the thrashing machine mentioned above is not an object of value for the self. Any egoism arising in connection with the thrashing machine depends on its nature and purpose. But that is different for each of the co-owners of the machine. For each of them is only interested in the thrashing of his own grain and not in the grain of the others. If he were interested in the others, his attitude would normally not be egoistic anymore. So the condition of the singularity of the immediate subject may remain unfulfilled. This holds only for those objecta for which the question of egoism, altruism, or neutrality remains undecided as long as they are considered in isolation. In connection with them, subjects may be accidentally cumulative. They can be easily differentiated from a plurality of immediate subjects of properly characteristic values for the self.

Externally, then, that is, according to its area of application, our description of egoism fulfills all reasonable conditions. Internally, however, according to its meaning, it approaches the natural, i.e. pregiven concept where the central position of the ego is reinstated, as it is indicated in the word "egoistic" itself. This, of course, can be interpreted as a return to a determination of egoism by means of the subject which had been given up in the beginning of this treatise. By the very fact that the ego is as much the subject / (p. 14) of an egoistic decision or valuation as of an altruistic decision or valuation it is clear that the subject is not the only important factor. On the other hand, it cannot be ignored - as we have seen - that the fact that something has several immediate subjects or merely one and again that this one subject is the ego or someone else depends essentially on the properties of the objectum. Thus, our characterization of egoism remains sufficiently objective.

---

[5] Compare **System der Werttheorie**, Vol. I, p. 79 f.

Section 3, Part I

Chapter Four

Altruistic and Neutral Value.

Value Position [*Wertstellung*]

In the foregoing chapters we succeeded in replacing our initial concept of egoism, which was founded on the concept of altruism[1], by an independent concept of egoism. Of course, now we are confronted with the problem of utilizing this newly acquired concept and determining, on its basis, the corresponding concepts of the altruistic and the neutral. As far as the concept of altruism is concerned, it seems to be most natural to analyze that concept in analogy to that of egoism. Then value, valuation, and desire should be called altruistic if the alter takes the same place as the ego in egoism, that is, if the alter is the only immediate subject. Without a doubt, this is too narrow. For if I work for the promotion of a certain discipline of the fine arts "in favor of" a person who is enthused by it, then my action is surely altruistic.

Nevertheless, a further difficulty may arise: do we have each time a case of altruism where a second subject provides proper mediation? For example, it can happen that E learns to esteem or even desire something simply because A esteems or desires it. In fact, this

---

[1] Compare (p. 4) above.

thing can easily become the object of a quarrel between E and A, where E is anything but altruistic. In the mean time I had the opportunity to point out at another place[2] that such extreme cases do not stand up to close scrutiny. For, at closer look, ego and alter are not faced with the same objectum of valuation. However, it cannot be doubted that the objectum / (p. 15) is the same when the alter influences subjectively the ego's valuation with his own valuation so that the ego values an objectum because the alter values it. In such a case there is usually no altruistic valuation. I have drawn the conclusion that the mutual relationship between the two subjects of valuation is not [sufficiently explained][3] by a value transfer. [The transfer alone is not important. But the _how_ of the transfer, that is, _how_ the valuations of the ego is mediated by the valuation of the alter, is essential. In the whole context of the transfer, the _position_ of the subject of valuation is important, which, in this respect, as has already been explained, is the "immediate" or "more remote" subject of valuation. In each egoistic valuation (also in altruism "for the sake of one's own advantage"), its subject is at once the immediate and even "exclusively immediate" subject of this valuation: the ego's valuation is joined] by a rather similar position of the alter which becomes apparent by the fact that the alter brings about the value relationship between the ego and the objectum in question. These two central positions are not yet completely analogous, as we can see. But they are sufficiently similar to justify the juxtaposition of egoism and altruism. The juxtaposition becomes apparent linguistically in the most significant way in which the preposition "for" (_für_) is used. This is also empirically instructive when the use of the term "for" is inspected. In general, it is first the value subject which is linguistically connected with the value objectum by the preposition "for." It is said of the objectum that it has value "for" this or that subject. However, "for" has a different and special meaning when we say of someone who was successful in a certain endeavor, "I am happy for him that he succeeded." Apparently, the "for" serves the special purpose here of pointing out the exceptional

---

2   Compare **Zur Grundlegung der allgemeinen Werttheorie**, III, par. 4 et al.

3   The text in brackets is missing in the original manuscript and is a translation of a proposed supplement by Prof. Franz Weber, Ljubljana. Karton XXX insert.

position held by the alter when the ego's attitude is altruistic. Then it is not too farfetched when we ascribe to the "for," in a phrase like "this is good for me," an analogous meaning when we consider the exceptional position of the ego in egoism.

The cases where either the ego or the alter occupies the just described central position are seen to be, already apriori, connected with those values, valuations, and desires where neither of the two possibilities applies. They are what I have called, years ago and again above[4], neutral values or "neutrality desires" *(Neutralbegehrungen)*. The similarity with the terms "neutrality value" *(Neutralwerte)* and "neutrality desires" *(Neutralbegehrungen)*[5] which were introduced above demands that they must be clearly separated in order to avoid misunderstandings.

The expressions "neutral value" and "neutrality value" are / (p. 16) legitimate because, in each case, the ego and the alter are excluded. However, the exclusion is not the same in each case. This is clear when we consider that, in spite of the exclusion, the ego remains the subject for the neutral value, but not at all for the neutrality value. The difference is so deep that the neutral value (and likewise neutral desire) can be characterized better from the standpoint of the ego than it can be by excluding the ego and the alter. [7] We found that for egoistic values the ego is the only immediate subject, and that for altruistic values the ego is a more remote subject and the alter is a closer, that is, more immediate subject. / (p. 17) However, for neutral values the ego is again the immediate subject, but not the only immediate subject. For there can be more of them, perhaps even an unlimited number.

The resulting difference can be called a difference in the value position of the subject regardless if we are dealing with values or desires. Then the division of values into egoistic, altruistic, and neutral values is a division according to the value position of possibly one and the same subject. However, the division of values into values for the self, values for the other, and neutrality values is strictly related to different subjects and is determined by the relative nature of the subjects. The

---

4   Comp. (p. 6).
5   Comp. (p. 3 f).

"artificial" definition of egoism and altruism with which I began the present discussion was given in the spirit of my earlier writings. In the description of egoism and altruism, it was kept closely to the objectum in question. Thus, it is contrasted with value for the self (*Selbstwert*), value for the other (*Fremdwerte*), and neutrality values which were divided according to the subject. The new characterization of egoistic, altruistic, and neutral values or desires stays closer to the subject than to the object, but it is more concerned with the value position of the subject. Thus, it is still clearly different from values for the self, values for the other, and neutrality values which are concerned with the nature of the subject.

A rather obvious consequence follows from the mutual relationship between the two divisions: what has just been called the value position of the subject can be applied to the ego as well as to the alter. We can speak of egoistic, altruistic, and / (p. 17) neutral values in connection with the ego as well as with the alter. Thus, not only value for the self but even value for the other can turn out to be egoistic, altruistic, or neutral. With sufficient orientation it has got to be the one as well as the other if the tripartition is a complete disjunction. The situation is different with neutrality values. They do not need an ego or alter, which is clear in connection with impersonal values. There it is meaningless to speak of egoism or altruism: neutrality values cannot be anything else but neutral values. Furthermore, when we speak of egoistic or altruistic values for the other, the ego, according to whom a value is determined as egoistic or altruistic, is different from the ego from whose standpoint the value is determined as value for the other. For here we are speaking of an ego which is someone other than the speaking or at least apprehending subject. The difference between egoistic and altruistic is made from the standpoint of the "other" ego.

Section 3, Part I

Chapter Five

Experience Values and Quality Values

(Erlebniswerte und Eigenschaftswerte) [8]

As stated above, the characterization of egoism, as given here, is without a doubt insufficient because nothing was said explicitly about the objects in question. Fortunately this insufficiency can be eliminated by determining the objecta in question by a simple disjunction which, however, must be given under a certain condition which has been pointed out before. We found[1] that the answer to the question if an attitude is egoistic or altruistic cannot be answered in connection with transferred values but only in connection with values in themselves *(Eigenwerte)* whereby the transfer values follow the nature of their parent values. From this point of view, the vast manifold of egoistic values seems, at first glance, extremely curtailed so that it is possible, as far as I can see, to differentiate distinctly between two types of egoistic values. [9] They are either experiences of the subject, relatively fleeting and temporary but in principle internally perceptible, or they are qualities of the subject, relatively long-lasting / (p. 18) but by nature not internally perceptible because they are not experiences but only dispositions for experiences. Feeling well or badly, a pleasant taste, a nauseating smell, a pleasant view, and many other psychic states belong to the first type. Health, illness, sharpness of the senses, susceptibility to pleasures or annoyances,

---

1 Comp. above (p. 13).

also taste for objects of art, intellectual and emotional capabilities, and many other properties belong to the second type of egoistic value objects. This justifies the division of egoistic values into experience values and quality values if, as it seems to me, there are no egoistic values for the self which cannot be subsumed under any of these two types and if egoistic transfer values are always subsumed under that type to which their parent values belong. So it can be seen at once that values of economics are usually counted among experience values. H. Schwarz, who must be credited, I think, with being the first to recognize the immense ethical importance of this division[2], uses the expressions "situational value" *(Zustandswert)* and "value for the person" *(Personwert).* But especially the expression "situational value" seems to be misleading insofar as "situation" designates mostly something of greater duration which, however, is frequently contrasted with a relatively durable "event" *(Vorgang)* in the same way as a constant is contrasted with a variable. However, the expression "value for the person" hit upon the essence of the matter in that it is far more concerned with the "person" of the subject than is "experience value" or "situational value." Moreover, it is concerned with the "personality" of the subject in that special sense which I tried to avoid when I suggested the term "personal value" *(persönlicher Wert)*[3]. But just because of this I would like to avoid speaking of "value for the person" over and beyond "personal value." After all, names matter little. In no way shall I ignore the part, but shall gratefully acknowledge it, which Schwarz played in our present choice of terms and in the development of our present investigations.

In the description of the two types of values which are already known / (p. 19) from direct experience, I must confine myself to a few remarks. When we speak of experience values, it is worth taking note of the fact that the term "experience" can be taken to be quite undefined. It may mean merely psychic experiences but it may also mean physical experiences. At least it is not clear why, e.g., an illness which is mostly understood to be of a physical nature should have only transfer value

---

[2] Comp. especially his excellent book **Das sittliche Leben**, Berlin, 1901, p. 36 f et al. and Ms. (p. 30).

[3] Comp. "Für die Psychologie und gegen den Psychologismus in der allgemeinen Werttheorie," **Logos**, Vol. III, 1912, p. 2.

and why the quality value should be saved for the organic sensations which are connected with it. Finally, one may be of the opinion that not all ends with sensation but that pleasure and displeasure are the last and proper experience values. This would agree with the ancient preconception that fundamentally pleasure is the only possible objectum of value and desire. This preconception, however, is quite obviously disproved by the occurrence of quality values and most transfer values. Even in connection with many experience values, data which are obviously experiential disprove the claim that, within the framework of those values, valuations are concerned with pleasures. It is only correct insofar that, externally considered, no experience seems to have value in itself *(Eigenwert)* which is not the cause of pleasure – if it is not itself already a pleasure. Internally considered, it is correct in that the pleasure which accompanies the experience is the mandatory motive for the valuation if it not the mandatory object itself. The motive retains its function as legitimating background of the valuation even if it is not the object of it. It can be shown inductively and convincingly that both cases hold. At the same time one can sense in them, as happens so often in emotional matters, a rationally comprehensible context which eludes initially clear understanding.

Even in quality values and experience values, which I have contrasted with each other above, the physical aspect cannot, in principle, be excluded. But it must be noted that is not as easy to accept psychic properties as objecta of values for the self as it is to accept physical properties as such. Seeing that the psychic aspect prevails we feel our attention drawn to the fact that the qualities in question are mainly dispositions. In respect to these dispositions / (p. 20) the very pressing question is raised if the value dependency of dispositions upon their correlates or results even allows for value in itself *(Eigenwert)*. A good memory is valued because remembering past events is valuable. Hypersensitivity to draughts or sense stimuli is taken to be anything but valuable because experiences which follow them or are occasioned by them are not valuable. So, in general we can say the value of qualities depends upon the value of the experiences in which they occur. Quality values are consequences of experience values and are similar to transferred values. The question now is with which justification they can be counted as values in themselves *(Eigenwerte),* as was done above. In fact, it cannot be denied that the value is transferred from the action to the dispositions. But that does not mean that this exhausts the total value of the disposition. That this indeed is not so will be clear, as will be seen[4] in the ethically significant fact that our attitude toward quality values is usually valued in a way quite different from our attitude toward experience values. When someone avoids bothersome or even painful therapy, say, an operation and lets an illness take its course even though he could be healed, his behavior is criticized as ethically weak and plaintive. Still, even today he who is *patiens frugus atque solem* has a claim to glory and no one will have justified objections against him. Such disregard for experience values is contrasted by a remarkable preference for quality values. For example, some people see the highest ethical ideal in the "culture of a person," and most people see in it at least something ethically very valuable.

Still, that the disposition is esteemed higher than examples of actions issuing from it can be understood on the basis of the relationship of transfer value to parent value insofar as there may be a sufficient parent value in the action flowing from the disposition in question. However, this is not applicable and does not hold if the value or valuation of the disposition has a prefix opposite / (p. 21) to that of the valuation of the action resulting from the disposition. The circumstances in which this actually may happen will be discussed later[5]. For the present it will suffice to mention that, for example, we highly esteem someone's conviction with which he is ready to sacrifice himself for the welfare and honor of the fatherland, but that we are far from wishing that the person in question will actually perish because of his conviction. In such a case and others of the same kind, the disposition reveals an unexpected independence from its results. This calls to mind the ancient question if a person is called good because most of his actions are good, or if the actions are good because they originate from a good person. The second part of the question does not contain a logical mistake, as we now clearly see. Direct experience does not admit any doubt that our valuations of convictions or beliefs are not exclusively – perhaps not even mainly –

---

4   Comp. Ms. (p. 20).
5   Comp. Ms. (p. 56 f).

based on our assessment of the actions ensuing from those beliefs. This can be understood in only one way, namely, that the disposition or, in short, the quality is related to the person. That is, the ego of the subject which is ignored in the experience itself. Here, we can ask whether there is a "value movement" *(Wertbewegung)* in Chr. v. Ehrenfels' sense[6], according to which values which were originally transferred values could become "derived"[7] values in themselves *(Eigenwerte).*

It would still remain a fact that, in comparison with valuations of experiences, the qualities remain sufficiently independent so that quality values can be contrasted with experience values as a special class of values in themselves.

[10] Under certain circumstances it is thinkable that the value of a quality is constituted by the value of the experience or that, on the other hand, the value of the experience is constituted by the value of the quality. Then they are treated accordingly. A second rather striking case occurs when someone puts great stock in reproducing this or that detail of a previous experience because it proves the reliability of his memory – or when a hunter is proud of the fact / (p. 22) that he sees a rabbit from a great distance and that he thus activated his sharpness of perception although he may not intend to actually hunt the rabbit. Here, the quality itself is valuable. Its value is transferred to the experience under an aspect which has been neglected so far, namely, the means of apprehension or knowledge of the value in this particular function receives its own albeit transferred value. The first of the just mentioned cases is theoretically less peculiar but more important; it illustrates the way in which quality values, in fact, can be demoted to the level of experience values. Anyone who wishes to be educated in the arts or in ethics focuses his attention normally on valuations of qualities for their own sake. But it happens sometimes that people study a musical instrument because they like to play a social role or want to earn applause or want to delight themselves in hours of leisure. It is even more refined when someone exercises his ethical talent in order to enjoy an enhanced self-esteem. None of these efforts will be valued too highly

---

6   Comp. his **System der Werttheorie**, Vol. I, Part Two.
7   Ibid., par. 44.

even though we hold the activity of that person in high esteem who strives for artistic or ethical ability as an aim in itself. Naturally the meaning and justification of contrasting experience values and quality values are not made questionable by such possible complications.

But first of all it is necessary to take a close look at experience and quality values in their relationship to egoistic values. For they have been differentiated in such a way that egoistic values can be better described. Examining direct experience we find at first– as far as I know and as has been mentioned – that the egoistic values in themselves (*Eigenwerte*) are either experience or quality values. I am not yet able to derive this result apriori from the nature of egoism. But it is my intuition that the peculiar relationship between objecta of egoistic values and the subject cannot be found anywhere else as far as one's experiences or qualities are concerned. However, the reverse is usually not the case. There, everything must be egoism which lies within the disjunction / (p. 23) of "experience value or quality value." The situation or quality of the apprehending subject does not determine if a value is an experience value or quality value; from the standpoint of this subject, it may be value for the other as well as value for the self. It is also possible that, among values for the self (*Selbstwerte*), there are, for the subject, experience values and quality values of such kind as belong to another person and are, therefore, altruistic values for the ego because they are values for another person. But they may also be neutral values. In the arts and sciences I may value experiences and capabilities of the alter without having to consider the alter's well-being. My own experiences and qualities can be considered in an analogous fashion; thus, the position "everything is egoistic which is either experience value or quality value" is not admissible.

At the same time, it has become clear that the contrast between experience value and quality value cannot be used for the description of altruism. The well-being of the alter, which alone is important here, may – as we know – be an egoistic, altruistic, or neutral well-being. In each of these cases we may be concerned with experiences as well as with qualities.

Section 3, Part II
The Subject Matter of Ethics
(A Characterization of Ethics)

Chapter Six

Values as Motives and Objects
of Theoretical Analysis

Ethics is dealing with value objects as such. There is no serious disagreement about that, although there may be various and different opinions about the character of that which constitutes the proper subject matter of ethics. Therefore, I thought, already years ago, that I should propose a value theoretical treatment of classic ethical problems[1]. I still hold that position. But I must revise the / (p. 24) overemphasis of this aspect to which I once adhered in keeping with old tradition[2]. But adherence to the old tradition has led us, in the past and also in the present, to unclear and even distorted conceptions of the task of ethical theory. The contrast originating from the formulation of the terms "theoretical science" and "practical science" which refer to the goal and operation of scientific work has long been a familiar thought. The contrast does not exclude in-between cases which originate from

---

[1] Comp. **Psychologisch-ethische Untersuchungen...**, p. 85 f, 216 ff.
[2] Ibid., p. 85.

theoretical studies extending into the practical domain[3]. For the characterization of this contrast, values had to be – at least more or less – taken into consideration. Theoretical studies are determined by the properties of objects; practical studies are determined by the values of objects. This may easily lead to the result that any time the value of an object is considered the consideration itself and also the theory within whose frame work the consideration takes place must be practical also. Therefore it has always been assumed to be a matter of course that ethics is a practical discipline of philosophy placed beside logic and aesthetics as companion disciplines[4]. What has been taken to be a matter of course, for a long time, revealed itself not to be at all a matter of course. For there is a science of values, namely the general theory of values which is a theoretical science, as no one will deny. Thus, it is indeed shown that a discipline does not have to be practical just because, in it, values are studied. If values – as cannot be doubted – are an important part of a practical science, then it is very important to know in what way values are the subject matter of that discipline; / (p. 25) and we must, in respect to this question, make painstaking inquiries.

As a rule one will not go wrong with the assumption that the extent of the role which values play in a science is an indication that values are its motive. The future physician studies the human body in its healthy and in its sick state. He does so in order to preserve and promote health and to fight disease. He wants to do so because health has (positive) value and disease has (negative) value. Thus, as value here pertains to a primarily physical life, it is agreed that there is a practical science with the general name "Medicine." Mostly, however, values are not even mentioned in connection with it. At least, they are not at all objects of its studies, neither in their general nature nor in their specific character. Still, they can be studied, as was seen quite clearly in the just-

---

3 On "theoretical - practical disciplines," comp. my discussions in "Über philosophische Wissenschaft und ihre Propädeutik," Wien, 1885, pp. 89 - 107, on practical - theoretical science, comp. Höfler in Martinak - Festschrift "Martinak als Pädagog und Pädagogiker" in **Beiträge zur Pädagogik und Dispositionstheorie**, ed. A. Meinong, Prag, Wien, Leibzig, 1919, p. 19 footnote.

4 Comp. my discussions in "Über die Stellung der Gegenstandstheorie im System der Wissenschaften," p. 116 f. (Also **Zeitschrift für Philosophie und philosophische Kritik**, Vol. CXXX, p. 14 f.)

mentioned theory of values. There, of course, values play a different role, and it is evident that a discipline which concerns itself with values from this point of view does not, for that reason, have to be a practical discipline. If we apply this to aesthetics and logic, which are not important for our present discussions, it is nevertheless immediately clear that, since beauty and truth are values in the proper sense of the word[5], logic and aesthetics are studied and practiced because of such values and in order to further such values. Without a doubt, these are practical disciplines, and it does not matter if that is of advantage or disadvantage for our goal. On the other hand, there is no reason why the affairs which are characterized and held together by the aforementioned aesthetic or logical values should not be studied theoretically specifically and because of that fact. The thus intended and growing theory cannot be denied the name of theoretical science.

This corresponds excellently with an aspect which, as a rule, occurs in the actual workings of these sciences. The manifestly practical ones among the practical disciplines exhibit a far greater theoretical character than the / (p. 26) "unprejudiced" pragmatic person might suspect. The representative of a science which concerns itself almost exclusively with the needs of everyday life frequently acts like the most esoteric theoretician[6]. To no one's surprise this happens most frequently where the expectations to favorably influence human actions are almost non-existent. In fact, anyone working in the domain of these sciences feels often enough that the emphasis on the "practical" is unnatural. Especially in logic, the emphasis on practicality may lead to the misunderstanding of the tasks which belong to this science and which, in principle, are surely practical. This label may have caused the relegation of certain problems to so-called "pure logic" which, quite some time later, were acknowledged to belong to the science of objects, that is, the "Theory of Objects[7]."

---

[5] Comp. **Über emotionale Präsentation (On Emotional Presentation)**, par. 15.

[6] Comp. "Über philosophische Wissenschaft und ihre Propädeutik" pp. 89 - 107.

[7] "Über die Stellung der Gegenstandstheorie im System der Wissenschaften," also **Zeitschrift für Philosophie und philosophische Kritik**, par. 20 ff.

It is easy now to apply our results to ethical theory with which we are really concerned here. Without a doubt, the good is ethically good, that is, it is valuable, and any practical discipline which intends to cultivate it is justified in doing so.

But our interest in the good is, at the same time, strong enough to prevail even in persons who arrived at the conviction in whatever way, that theoretical deliberations are incapable of influencing the behavior of people. The person who does not study ethics anymore as a practical discipline does not lose his justification for his activity. Frequently he may theoretically pursue his interest in ethics without stopping to consider skeptically if his theoretical results can be actualized – even only in principle. For him, anyone's belief that he works in the service of practical goals appears to be contrived.

In summary, the following can be stated: the answer to the question whether the inclusion of values in a science makes it practical or not depends upon why values were introduced, out of theoretical "interest in them" or out of practical "interest for them." In the latter case the value constitutes a motive, in the former case it is the object of theoretic analysis. Thus, / (p. 27) ethics can be, but does not have to be, studied as a practical discipline. Anyone who, against the beliefs of pragmatism, feels that the interest in an object for its own sake and not as a means for an end constitutes a privilege of dignity *(Dignität)* should also believe that ethics is degraded when it is classified as merely a practical discipline.

Section 3, Part II
The Subject Matter of Ethics

Chapter Seven

Rational and Empirical Elements in Ethics. A Few Thoughts Concerning Its Method

Naturally, ethics as apriori science does not depend upon one's treating it as practical or theoretical. Every empirical science, even in its most underdeveloped form, looks for and finds its portion of apriori knowledge. On the other hand, a science of values, even one with the highest rational aspirations, will treat the initially arising question whether this or that object has value by looking at actual valuations and by answering the question empirically. That does not mean that anything which in fact is valued does in fact have value in any sense of the term. I may have gone too far, in the past, when I declared that value laws which I had established were all taken from experience[1]. The basis of my statements were doubtlessly experiences of the ethical conduct of modern civilized man which are accessible to any educated person. Pre-scientific word meanings testify to such experiences and

---

[1] **Psychologisch-ethische Untersuchungen ...**, p. 92 ff.

should be utilized as much as possible by ethical theory. [11] At the same time an inner reasonableness of the empirically established valuations can be found and, therefore, also a rational aspect. And these provide a legitimatization for the empirical results. Whenever primitive value laws are formulated and substantiated, concepts do play a role which – regardless of how empirical they are – are not / (p. 28) determined by mere induction but stand for the schematic simplification of that which in reality is incomprehensibly variable and complicated. The same holds for any other theory. For example, the "Law of Omission," of which I shall speak in greater detail soon[2], must not be understood in such a way that the omission of something believed to be meritorious is held by everybody to be admissible, and that the omission of something believed to be correct is held by everybody to be reprehensible. It should not be taken in such a way that, for everybody, the value change in an action goes hand in hand with a value change in the corresponding omission. Moreover, it remains possible that, in connection with empirical valuations, the Law of Omission can occasionally be violated – however, with the reservation that the one committing the violation is wrong. To be "correct" or "right" does not have to be rational. It becomes rational only with explicit exclusion of empirical interpretation.

If I am correct in saying that ethical knowledge begins with experience, then it is hardly astounding that one cannot hold it against ethics when our "principles" are much less known than that which is, under favorable conditions, derived from them[3]. Our human capability of comprehension breaks down when it is fed too much or too little information; it breaks down *vis a vis* the extremely general and also the extremely particular. As in all other fields, so likewise in philosophy and especially in ethics: the middle is most accessible and therefore functions as the pre-given; and it is the task of scientific research to advance beyond the "given." [12] This even holds of the ground from which apriori knowledge has always reaped its richest harvest, that is, mathematics, as became evident in the recent labors over its principles.

---

2 Comp. p. 124, (p. 30) ff.
3 Contrary to L. Nelson **Ethische Methodenlehre**, Leipzig, 1915, reissued as **Kritik der praktischen Vernunft**, Leipzig, 1917, Vol. I, pp. 5 ff.

This is especially true where empirical or, rather, inductive procedures must proceed from relatively concrete cases and aim at the universal as its research goal which is relatively unknown, and the access to it is the result / (p. 29) of scientific labor. It is a peculiar feature of the theories of value, especially of ethics, that the facts from which they proceed are valuations. The "principles" for which we are searching do not appear explicitly in those valuations themselves. Thus, the certainty of those valuations, on the basis of those "principles," remains at best a matter of consent. It is hardly justified, then, to erect on these foundations a methodology of ethics, as has recently been done[4]. Neither the applied acuteness nor the excellent presentation by the author can reconcile us with the theoretically questionable character of this methodology.

Naturally, this does not preclude that the peculiarity of the ethical subject matter carries with it peculiar appropriate methods which have been codified as methodological theses and which deserve continued attention in the course of further ethical research. Thus, I myself felt compelled to accept a certain procedure for the solution of the primitive but also fundamental problem of how to determine exactly the proper objects of ethics. Basically it has been nothing but a specialization of a procedure which has been called "method of changes of accompanying circumstances" *(Methode der Begleitveränderungen)* since J. St. Mill. In order to determine what is the proper object of value and what is, therefore, the object of ethics, it was accepted as the most natural procedure to determine first what it is that gradually changes in the objecta in question whenever their ethical value gradually changes. It was initially expected that the problem could best be solved by concentrating on the central area of ethics which is fairly well laid out by the contrary terms "good" and "bad" and which I took, following convention, as the domain of the specifically "moral" in contrast with the more general domain of the ethical[5]. In this context I looked especially for laws which are exhibited in moral values. For that purpose I found such facts especially useful where the altruistic and egoistic feelings of the acting or, at least, willing person come into conflict with each other and where the magnitude of the active altruism

---

4   Ibid., pp. 57 ff.
5   **Psychologisch-ethische Untersuchungen ...**, p. 88.

is measured by the egoism which the person has to overcome or / (p. 30) which he cannot overcome[6]. The procedure which yielded, as we may suppose, quite favorable results within a limited field was applied by H. Schwarz to a much wider domain[7] which, in a certain sense, is the totality of ethics. The good results which were, thus, obtained deserve consent in their main points even from a writer who cannot agree with many psychological or value theoretical statements of this deserving author[8]. Under these circumstances it would please me immensely if the following small contributions, which utilize Schwarz' main results as a basis from which they proceed, should be judged by the creditable colleague to be a step forward in the direction which he took.

---

[6] Ibid., par. 49 ff.

[7] Especially in the important book **Das sittliche Leben**, Berlin, 1901. The character of his statements reveals the role which my **Psychologisch-ethische Untersuchungen zur Werttheorie** played in them, which is also substantiated by the gratifying agreement with me which the esteemed author previously had shown in his **Ethik** (Schnurpfeils Volksbibliothek, Nr. 51-52, pp. 45 ff, Leipzig) by a detailed account of my discussions.

[8] Comp. especially W. Liel, "Gegen eine voluntaristische Begründung der Werttheorie," Nr. X of **Untersuchungen zur Gegenstandstheorie und Psychologie**, Leipzig, 1904, edited by me.

Section 3, Part III
The Law of Omission [13]

Chapter Eight

Two Objections.
Answer to the First Objection

We want to keep as closely as possible to **Psychologische-ethische Untersuchungen,** and we also want to preserve the simplicity of the subject matter. In the following, therefore, I want to limit my thinking to that which I call specifically "moral" with the reservation, however, that the application of my ideas may be enlarged later. I shall begin a little prematurely to devote some thought to the "Law of Omission," as I once labeled it. According to this law each point on the plus line of moral values above zero corresponds to a minus point below / (p. 31) zero in such a way that whenever the first indicates the value of a commission (*Setzung*), the second indicates the value of its omission. When the four main classes of moral value objects are considered, they, together with the foregoing, lead to the previously mentioned thesis[1] that the omission of the meritorious is admissible and that the omission of the correct is reprehensible and vice versa. No one has doubted the actual validity of this law, as far as I know: the law is empirically partially

---

[1] See p. 124 (p. 30).

verified by actual valuations. Its precision, which goes beyond experience, results from the appropriate process of making concepts precise and well-differentiated from each other. Still, there are some problems left which must be solved theoretically, and, in the following, I will contribute some efforts to their solution.[2] [14]

First of all, two items must be pointed out by virtue of which our law seems to create paradoxa that give rise to the doubt whether the law is correctly formulated. Firstly, the value zero point can be exceeded in such a way that a decision of a morally extremely high positive value (*Überwert*) not only loses its extremely high value through an appropriate modification (that is, receives the value zero), but, beyond that, acquires a negative value. Upon the question in which way such a modification of an action changes the value of the corresponding omission, the Law of Omission yields the answer: when the value of an action approaches zero as a limit, the value of the omission approaches infinity with the opposite prefix as the limit. The movement of the value of an action from a positive point on the line across zero to a negative point corresponds, in the case of its omission, at first, to a value which moves to a negative infinite, but, then, after a jump to a positive infinite, again to a finite but positive value. With continuity on one side, is the discontinuity on the other side believable which consists in changing abruptly from a negative infinite to a positive infinite?

Secondly, the apparent incompatibility of the situation with a law / (p. 32) does not seem to be rational. The law concerns counter-feelings (*Gegengefühle*)[3] which seem to be, at first glance, a subject matter of empirical psychology. However, it in turn can be founded on an apriori value law. Everyone has experienced sorrow over the loss or non-existence of an object when the existence of that object pleased him very much – and vice versa. This seems to be universally accepted. However, in reality this is not always true[4]. Thus, the rational law which was mentioned a short while ago appears at the center of the matter. It is

---

[2] The need for this impressed itself on me during our very stimulating discussions in the philosophical seminar in Graz at the end of the winter semester of 1917.

[3] Ad counter-feelings compare **Zur Grundlegung der allgemeinen Werttheorie**, III, par. 2.

[4] **Über Annahmen II**, p. 308.

clear that the Law of Omission does not conform with what is taken to be obvious. The omission of something meritorious, that is, highly valuable, results in an admissible, that is, slightly negative *(unterwertig)* value; the omission of a correct action which is of a merely moderate value results in something reprehensible which is of considerable negative value. Within each of the four classes, the omission of a more valuable action results in a fact of smaller negative value, and vice versa. The question is whether the Law of Omission can be retained in spite of these discrepancies.

As happens in so many cases, the seemingly more radical of the two difficulties was, at closer look, easily recognized as unproblematic. Functions which are discontinuous, at some places, are not unheard of. The change from negative infinite to positive value occurs, for example, in the trigonometric tangent of an angle which increases beyond 90°. In our case, there is even another point of view under which this paradox, which will always be there, appears in a mild light. As seen in the example of the tangent, the paradox is timeless. But where we are concerned with reality and especially with the course of time, it may seem very strange when the continuous course of that which is independently variable is correlated with the discontinuous course of that which is dependently variable. This would be the case in the moral domain if we succeeded in modifying a decision continuously in its specific determinations in such a way, or subject it to any modification in such a way, that the value zero point is crossed; that is, the high positive value is converted into a negative value, or vice versa. With analogous changes of the correlated omissions, the abrupt change / (p. 33) must in fact be accomplished or at least thought to be accomplished; and that is not an easy matter. Even if my characterization of high positive and negative moral values, which I had attempted in the past, is in principle correct[5], one cannot think that a conversion from a positive value to a negative values is possible in the sense just described. Thus, the aspect of the Law of Omission with which one may take greatest offense, is eliminated.

---

[5] **Psychologisch-ethische Untersuchungen...**, p. 91.

Section 3, Part III
The Law of Omission

Object Theoretic Interpretation of the Law of Omission

Chapter Nine

The Law of Omission and
the Principle of Double Negation

The second difficulty is so hard to overcome that it seems appropriate to return to it in a later context.[1] Because of the Law of Omission, another task must be taken on within the theory of values. The theory is contrasted in such a curious manner with the matter just discussed that the Law of Omission emerges as something unproblematic, which gives rise to the question whether this law is a special case of a more general law which is rational and a part of object theory. If we succeed in exhibiting this connection, then we will not only obtain deeper insight into the Law of Omission but will contribute to the advance of object theoretic knowledge. In this connection it does not matter if the essence of the Law of Omission might be found in the principle of double nega-

---

[1] Comp. p (?) below. (No reference found, the eds.)

tion or in something which is analogous to that principle. One might
think that the omission of an omission would result in a commission, as
the negation of a negation results in an affirmation, and that, in fact,
not only the omission of something correct is itself reprehensible but that
the omission of the omission of the correct is itself correct. But it is seen
immediately that the analogy between omission and negation can break
down, especially when it is a double omission. We may speak of an
omission when / (p. 34) there is an opportunity for doing something, or at
least for wanting to do something, and the opportunity passes unused.
For no act of willing occurred, or the agent is opposed to that which could
be realized by his willing (according to his opinion, of course). Perhaps
it is easier to connect the first of these possibilities with negation than the
second of the possibilities. In respect to the first possibility, it will not do
to even consider its possible omission. Although there cannot be an
omission of an omission, in this case the Law of Omission itself is without a doubt applicable. But it is striking that the principle of negation is
effective over a narrower domain than the law of omission. This
becomes already apparent in the first step of the first and the second
possibility and not at the second step. That is, it becomes apparent when
the meritorious is omitted and becomes permissible (*zulässig*). No
occasion is as yet given for double negation or anything analogous to
double negation. Moreover, it need not be mentioned that the characteristics of the four value classes or the gradations of values themselves
are not lost in the problem of negation.

Section 3, Part III
The Law of Omission

Chapter Ten

Analogies of the Law of Omission

Our theory will achieve considerable gain when we consider that the four classes of moral values, in view of the series which they make up and in view of the manner in which the members of the series are connected by the Law of Omission, are analogous to groups of quadruples which are completely different from them and also from each other. It has recently been shown by object theoretical analysis[1] that some of the groups of quadruples have related characteristics. One hopes, therefore[2], that this knowledge will support value theoretic ethics. At this place I want to mention some groups which are relevant in this connection.

The "forms" of "categorical judgments" which have / (p. 35) been discussed over and over in traditional formal logic were usually labeled A, E, I, and O; they form, in the series "A, I, O, E," an ordered series. This is clear when we consider that the "some" with which I and O are dealing include a quantitative series from zero to "one, several, many" (up to "all" as a limit). I and O meet at the zero point and run,

---

[1] Comp. A. Höfler, "Abhängigkeitsbeziehungen zwischen Abhängigkeitsbeziehungen," **Sitzungsberichte der K. Akademie der Wissenschaften in Wien**, phil. hist. section, Vol. CLXXXI 1917, esp. p. 45.

[2] Ibid., p. 51 footnote.

ordered in relation to each other, in opposite directions. Thus, all four terms can be pictured on a straight line which, toward the center, shows I and O with the zero point between them, and A and E at the outer ends. Some of the relations which hold between these four terms are treated traditionally as the "logical square." A systematic and exhaustive study had to wait until A. Höfler[3] tackled it[4]. We are primarily interested in what has been traditionally called the relation of contradiction which holds between the first and third and between the second and fourth term. Thereby, we take the just-mentioned linear series of the terms for granted. If it is denied that all S is P, then it is given simultaneously that some S is not P and vice versa. If it is not the case that at least some S is P, no S is P and vice versa. The analogy between these relationships and those given by the Law of Omission is evident.

A. Höfler showed convincingly[5] that the same dependencies which hold between A, I, O, and E also hold between "must-be-done, may-be-done, does-not-have-to-be-done, may-not-be-done" (*Müssen, Können, Nichtmüssen, Nichtkönnen*). These four objects also constitute an ordered series in the just-given sequence. In that series again, two pairs of members separated by an immediate neighboring member are connected in analogy to the Law of Omission. The situation is not quite the same with the series "same, similar, not-the-same, dissimilar[6]" or with "commanded (ordered), permitted, not-commanded (not ordered), forbidden[7]" (*geboten, erlaubt, nicht geboten, verboten*). The following groups of four are further examples of many real or apparent analogies of the Law of Omission: / (p. 36) "certain, presumable, presumably-not, certainly-not" (*gewiss vermutlich, vermutlich nicht, gewiss nicht*); "necessary, contingent, contingently-not, necessarily-not" (*notwendig, zufällig, zufällig nicht, notwendig nicht*); "lavishness, generosity, thrift, avarice" (*Verschwendung, Freigebigkeit, Sparsamkeit, Geiz*); "revenue, savings, expenditure, waste"

---

3 Ibid., p. 13 ff.
4 Comp. also W. Frankl, "Gegenstandstheoretische Beiträge zur Lehre vom sogenannten logischen Quadrat," **Archiv für systematische Philosophie**, Vol. XIII. pp. 346 ff.
5 Höfler, ibid. pp. 18 ff, 46 f.
6 Ibid., p. 46.
7 Ibid., p. 52 footnote.

(*Einnahme, Ersparniss, Entgang, Ausgabe*); "abundance, sufficiency, not-too-much, too-little[8]" (*Überfluss, genug, nicht zuviel, zu wenig*). The list can easily be continued. The following question is pressing: What can be learned from these results concerning the character of the Law of Omission?

Naturally, we must first establish what the cases which are parallel to the Law of Omission have in common in spite of their differences. A. Höfler[9] pointed out that among the members of the quadruples two are always the negation of the other two, and two are always precision objects whereas the other two are not precision objects but are approximations of precision objects. The following thought may get us a few steps ahead: the second and, in some respects, the most important part of the parallel cases, the group of modal determinations has been studied in great detail[10]. It may be assumed that the results of these studies can be applied to the other groups. It is, therefore, recommended that we take a closer look at the modal series.

---

8 The last three examples were brought up during the seminar sessions which were mentioned in Ms. (p. 31) footnote.

9 Ibid., p. 49.

10 Comp. my book **Über Möglichkeit und Wahrscheinlichkeit**, especially Par. 16.

Section 3, Part III
The Law of Omission

Chapter Eleven

The Modal Series as
Double Series of Potiores

It is relatively unimportant that, in the light of the mentioned studies[1], the kind of necessity which is traditionally called "must" (*Müssen,* perhaps "obligation") at closer look does not really belong here. For the possibility given with the expression "can" is correlated with actuality. This yields a relation which may have become obscured by the fact that the rational was given a preferred position in most relevant and important studies. There, the apriori possibility was joined by an apriori factuality. / (p. 37) And necessity which is characteristic of apriori possibilities [15] may become more apparent so that we rather speak of necessity than of necessary factuality. Whatever holds of the term "necessity" holds of the term "impossibility" when it is understood rationally, as is frequently done. Strictly speaking, the proper members of our group of four are actuality-of-being, possibility-of-being, possibility-of-not-being, actuality-of-not-being. If this terminology is accepted, then the most striking aspects of the series are easily seen.

---

[1] Comp. **Über Möglichkeit und Wahrscheinlichkeit**, p. 121 ff.

The series or line is divided into two halves, one concerning being, the other concerning not-being. The two halves meet at the zero point or infactuality. The zero limit indicates that the two half lines are quantitative lines. Furthermore, they are characterized by the fact that, within each of the lines, a law holds which I have called the "law of the potius." According to this law, wherever it holds, the givenness of something larger implies the givenness of something smaller. Moreover, the two half lines are joined together by the "law of complements" according to which each possibility of not-being coincides with a possibility of being. Both complement each other and amount to that totality which is considered to be a unity in the usual symbolism of the calculus of possibilities and probabilities. I have tried[2] to illustrate the law in the double line of possibilities in which, by the way, each of the half lines by itself constitutes a spatial image[3] of the manifold of points in question. However, it is at most conventional to place the coinciding points closely below each other and it is not meant to be a two-dimensional spatial image[4]. In the sense of our discussion, the manifold of modal determinations is labeled "double line (or series) of potiores." Then the question arises whether the instances of lawfulness referred to by this expression / (p. 38) can make the following relationships clear: between factuality-of-being and possibility-of-not-being, and between the possibility-of-being and the factuality-of-not-being.

Let us assume that a being has the possibility of three quarters. Then it follows from the law discussed here that its opposite, the not-being in question, is of the possibility one quarter. But we must be permitted to presuppose, according to ordinary language, that whatever is of three-quarter possibility is of "primary possibility" (*Hauptmöglichkeit*) or, as we may say more generally, is a "potissimum," that is, occupies a point in the series of potiores for which there is no further potius under the circumstances at hand. If there were a further potius, then the coinciding greater opposite possibility would have to be lower. However, let us

---

2 Ibid., p. 95.
3 Concerning the principle of images, comp. ibid., pp. 100 ff.
4 Symbolism representing space has different tasks, as e.g. in the "logical square" or in A. Höfler's "modal square" (compare "Abhängigkeitsbeziehungen...," ibid, p. 46 f.). It is not appropriate to consider my double line a modification of the square. (Ibid., p. 53.)

assume that, contrary to our assumption above, there is no three-quarter possibility, then there would still be an opposite one-quarter possibility. But it would be overshadowed by the fact that there would still be a greater possibility for this opposite whereby the potissimum would be close to one quarter but would also be situated in a remote position on the half line of the possibilities-of-not-being. The same holds, of course, for all the other members of our double line of potiores not counting the two zero points. Their exceptional position consists in this, that the law of the potius does not apply to them. But the previous consideration of the three quarter possibility does not apply either, because the absence of a zero possibility is incompatible with the absence of a higher possibility. Now, if we leave the two zero points of our double series out of consideration, then the upper limits of each half line, i.e. factuality, can be differentiated from the line of possibilities. Let us designate factuality-of-being with I, the possibility-of-being with II, the possibility-of-not-being with III, and the factuality-of-not-being with IV. Then the following can be stated: if I does not hold, then there is at least some counter coincidence of some degree of infactuality. This is something which belongs to the domains III and IV, and in the latter case even a potiori to III. If II does not hold, only IV can hold. An analogous case holds if we proceed, instead from the one half line, / (p. 39) from the other half line, namely III and IV. In summary we can say: if I, II, III, IV are not the case, then respectively III, IV, I, II are the case. This is nothing but a consequence of the law which describes the double line of potiores. At the same time it is a clear analogy of the Law of Omission.

Section 3, Part III
The Law of Omission

Chapter Twelve

Analogous Cases Which Are to Be Understood as Double Series of Potiores

It is now clear that the agreement of the other quadruple groups with each other and with the Law of Omission can be taken for granted. However, we must succeed in ascertaining that double lines of potiores do occur in them.

That this should be easy, especially in respect to the certainty - uncertainty series, may be concluded from the close relationship holding between uncertainty and possibility which I have explained at another place[1]. Of course, it is clear that not each and every subjectively qualified certainty and uncertainty can be used as an analogous case of the Law of Omission. When someone does not apprehend an objective with certainty, it does not follow that he understands the opposite objective. In the same sense, if he does understand the opposite objective, it does not follow that a judgment is made with certainty. Rather, it is a

---

1   Comp. **Über Möglichkeit und Wahrscheinlichkeit**, p. 56 ff.

justified certainty and presumption; or more precisely, he is justified to make a judgment with certainty or a presumptive judgment. It may be proposed that our law holds rather for truth and probability than for certainty and presumption. But, as is readily seen, this is not true either. If it is not true that A is B, then it is not the probability of the opposite but its truth which follows. Special complications arise which originate from the relationship of probability to pure and applied possibility[2]. As peculiar as it may seem, the domain of our law lies in the middle between the extremely subjective and the extremely objective, and, thus, refers to a sphere of personal probabilities[3]. If I am not certain / (p. 40) of an objective in a sense that my understanding, that is, the knowledge at my disposal, does not permit me to make a justified judgment of certainty, then this knowledge makes it legitimate to hold that the opposite is to some degree probable. Within these limits the double series of potiores is in fact applicable.

Without a doubt, the same is the case with the series A, I, O, E, even though they are discontinuous whereas the modalities are continuous. The determination "all" is certainly the potius of the determination "some." And whatever holds of many, apotiori also holds of "a few" and "one." It is likewise understood that the law of coinciding complements holds with the same clarity, even though the total amount to which the coinciding determinations complement each other is not constant for different series for the reason that the "all" under consideration may be a greater or smaller number of individuals. The traditional determinations of "quantity" are opposite objectives in the same way as the being or not-being of modalities, in the widest sense of the word, especially being thus-and-so and not being thus-and-so. In fact, the following law holds: with the not-being of a point of the one half line the being of a counter coincident, however close, but different point of the same half line is given, and it is situated between the first point and the zero point of the half line. And the first point is its potius. The law of "contradiction" which connects I and III and II and IV, under the presumption of similar designations, is only a special case of the just-described situation.

---

2   Comp. ibid., 484 ff.
3   Comp. ibid., 533.

In the domain of that which A. Höfler called fittingly
"*Gleichungsrelationen*" ("relations of equalities"(?))[4], the clarity of the
situation is impaired by unsolved problems in the theory of objects[5]. But
following R. Ameseder's investigations we can say that much[6]: there is
always a necessary concurrence of two opposite relations to which the
terms "similarity" and "difference" / (p. 41) can be applied. The meaning of the terms "dissimilarity" and "inequality" still remain to be
stipulatively defined. On the other hand, it is clear that "equality"
means the maximum of similarity which coincides with the zero point of
dissimilarity. Thus, greater similarities belong to smaller differences,
and smaller similarities belong to greater differences. As a result, it
cannot be doubted that the greater similarity or the greater difference are
the potius of lesser similarity or lesser difference. It can be seen at once
that relationships between I and III and between II and IV hold which
correspond to the Law of Omission.

---

4   "*Abhängigkeitsbeziehungen zwischen Abhängigkeitsbeziehungen,*" et ibid.,
     p. 46.
5   Comp. R. Ameseder, "Beiträge zur Grundlegung der Gegenstandstheo-
     rie," #II of **Untersuchungen zur Gegenstandstheorie und Psycholo-
     gie**, Leipzig, 1904, pp. 101 ff, edited by me.
6   Ibid., pp. 95 ff.

Section 3, Part III
The Law of Omission

Chapter Thirteen

Analogous Cases of a Different Kind

The quadruple referred to by the terms "commanded, permitted, not-commanded, forbidden" *(geboten, erlaubt, nicht geboten verboten)* leads us to the value theoretical or ethical domain. [16] This becomes especially apparent when we use concepts in an objective sense which have been so far subjective. This results in the series "must-be, may-be, may-not-be, must-not-be" *(sein sollen, sein dürfen, nicht-sein dürfen, nicht-sein sollen)*. In shorter, but rather unclear terms, one can speak of "must-not" and "may-not" *(nicht sollen, nicht dürfen)*. For "must-not" *(nicht sollen)*, and analogously "not-want-to" *(nicht wollen)*, may be, in the exact sense of the word, the negativum of "must," but in an inexact meaning of the word, the "must" of the opposite and finally the negative "must" are meant as the opposite to the positive "must" *(Sollen)*[1]. "May" *(Dürfen)* functions in an analogous fashion. In order to make the variety of our material clearer symbols should be employed. The lack of a "must" *(Sollen)* (S) or "may" *(Dürfen)* (D) is designated by zero. The quality of S and D stands to the left of the symbol; the quality of

---

[1] Comp. **Über emotionale Präsentation (On Emotional Presentation)**, pp. 162 ff.

being as an object appears on the right side of the symbol. Then it may be sufficient to designate the merely negative quality with a minus sign. The positive quality may remain undesignated. Then we get, at once, the following ordered series.

S	D	O	-D	-S
-S-	-D-	O	D	-S-

The neighboring symbols on the vertical lines indicate objective situations which coincide objectively and by their nature, even though they may not coincide subjectively according to our behavior. For our purposes it is sufficient / (p. 42) to concentrate on the upper series. It is familiar to us because there is a series of potiores on the right and on the left of the zero. Whatever one must do one always may do. In an analogous fashion, one can do what one must do. Thus, we may expect that the two half lines which constitute the horizontal series can be superimposed and that, in this way, coinciding points can be found which again result in a double series of potiores. The analogy of the Law of Omission is again explained in the usual manner.

In the meantime, the analogous cases of must and can, or rather of factuality and possibility, break down: according to this analogy S would be a point and D a line. But the must (S) here is capable of intensification, whereas it is not natural to speak of degrees of may (D). It would be rather arbitrary to assign to may (D) even a short line, perhaps close to zero. This would make the success of the superimposition questionable since the may of being and the may of not-being should coincide. However, there are no reservations against the concurrence of must-be with the absence of any must-be of opposite quality: it is even less evident why the lack of positive must-be should coincide with a negative must-be. All in all, we can see that subsuming the whole situation under the point of view of the double series of potiores will only create insurmountable difficulties. The theory must realize this and take different routes.

The new route can be found once we see, after closer inspection, that the word "may" (*Dürfen*) designates an object of negative quality. I am not ignoring the danger, especially after I made so many of my own mistakes, that an object which by its nature is positive is taken to be negative because it can be converted into a precise concept by way of negation. At closer look it cannot be ignored that we do something because it is not forbidden, that is, must-not deserves to be negated. If this is really the case then, for the time being, the above series of five members has in reality only three members:

$$S \qquad O \qquad -S$$

The terms S and -S constitute, in their degrees of intensity, each a half series ending at zero. On the other hand, D or -D are defined as / (p. 43) that part of the series which remains after the serial part -S or S is subtracted. Essentially D is either O or -S. Likewise -D is essentially only O or S. Let us call S "I," D "II," -D "III," and S "IV." Then the following results obtain immediately: if I is not, III is; if II is not, IV is, and vice versa. The situation here is exactly as it is with the Law of Omission and the double series of potiores. Only the underlying reasons are different. We still have a series in the gradations of S and -S, but it is not a double series. Strictly speaking, D and -D are not members of the same series anymore. It is clear that what just has been said holds likewise for "commanded, allowed, forbidden." For the lawful relationships of I, II, III, and IV should be insisted upon with each complete series which contains a point of indifference. The same should be expected with any triple A, B, C if the concepts of non-A and non-C have been formulated beforehand as limited to this group.

In a similar fashion we cannot recur to the double series of potiores in connection with the examples which were studied when the question was raised whether they were analogous to the Law of Omission. Even in respect to them we must be satisfied with a substitute, namely negations which were introduced by definition. First, this is the case with the series which goes from abundance (*Überfluss*) to deficiency (*Mangel*), from the too-much to too-little. Anything belonging to this series is available goods or values (valuables), for which there must be a limit which demand (*Bedarf*) cannot exceed. There is another limit below which the supply may not drop without lagging behind the demand. Let us formulate, by negation, the concepts of the not-too-much and not-too-little. Thus, we get the four-member series "too-much, not-too-little, not-too-much, too-little" in respect to which one question must still be answered, namely whether the middle members could rather be or, at least, could as well be given in reverse sequence. In fact, the "too-much" and "not-too-much" naturally exclude each other. The same holds for "too-little" and "not-too-much." Let us assign the numerals I to IV to the members of the series. Then the validity of the four cases which are analogous to the Law of Omission is immediately clear by definition. / (p. 44) The same consideration can be applied to those two series of which one leads from waste to avarice, the other from revenue *(Einnahme)* to waste *(Ausgabe)*. The first can be taken for a special case of the series "too-much - too-little." The characteristics which seem to be distributed over the series seem to be attitudes of giving. In respect to these attitudes, all four types which were to be determined above have already been designated by traditional expressions. Whoever gives too much is wasteful, whoever gives too little is miserly, whoever does not give too much may be thrifty, whoever does not give too little may even be called generous. Thus, the well known relations between the terms I to IV are guaranteed. The second series concerns the changes in mobile goods *(bewegliche Güter)*, especially money. When such goods are growing, it is revenue; when they diminish, it is waste *(Ausgabe)*. If an expected revenue fails to realize, it is expenditure *(Entgang)*. If an expected waste does not occur, then it is savings *(Ersparnis)*, and expenditure and savings are nothing but the failing of revenue and waste to occur. The order "revenue, savings, expenditure, waste" is legitimate by virtue of the relationship given in the prefixes. In I and II the prefixes are positive; in III and IV they are negative. Thus, the relations are guaranteed.

Lastly, we must consider an example which, now and previously, unavoidably relates to necessity. There, the series "necessity-of-being, contingency-of-being, contingency-of-not-being, necessity-of-not-being" is formed where "being" (in a wide sense of the word) can also be understood as "being" in the narrower sense of the word and also as being thus-and-so. This quadruple group has been mentioned with the sole intention of illustrating that a situation which in general seems to resemble the examples under consideration here does not have to be analogous to the Law of Omission. And it is important to us that it may not hold at all. When an objective is called contingent as far as it is factual but not necessary[2], and when the four members of our series are again given in the sequence I - IV then it is clear that III does not follow from the not-being *(Nichtbestand)* of I, and that IV does not follow from the not-being of II. If it is not necessary that B is, then the opposite does not have to be contingent *(zufällig)*, because it could even be necessary and also because A could contingently be B if it is not necessarily B which is incompatible / (p. 45) with the belief that it is contingently not B. Likewise when A's being B is not contingent, then the opposite does not have to be necessary but may also be contingent. One could attempt to save the law by defining contingency without reference to factuality, that is, each objective which is not necessary is contingent. But this does not seem to help, for also in that case one cannot infer the being of III from the not-being of I, because an objective which is not necessary does not entail that its opposite is also not necessary. On the other hand, our law does hold if the grouping of the four members as was done above is changed. If we really take contingency to be the negation of necessity then in fact the not-being of I implies III, the not-being of II implies IV. But the new group cannot claim to be an ordered series.

---

[2] Comp. **Über Möglichkeit und Wahrscheinlichkeit**, p. 240.

Section 3, Part III
The Law of Omission

Chapter Fourteen

A General Characterization of
Analogous Cases.
Polar Opposites

Let us look again at our preceding analyses. We notice that some of the quadruples, which follow the analogy of the Law of Omission, clearly carry with them the characteristics of the double series of potiores whereas, at first, the others do not seem to have these characteristics. Is it possible that the properties which were immediately obvious in the first quadruples can also guide us in unearthing criteria in the second groups by which – and also from the very character of the pertinent situation – their lawful behavior could become evident? It may be well advised to return to the first cases, namely the double series of potiores, and study them in greater detail.

First of all, we will pay closer attention to the nature of those objects to which a double series of potiores applies. The danger prevails that this attempt will yield, at first, quite modest results. The two halves of a double series of potiores are apparently constituted of the determinates of an object / (p. 46) which can be determined and is, thus, undetermined or incomplete[1]. This object is obviously the opposite of the corresponding object on the other half of the series which is likewise and in the same way incomplete. The opposite in question is not that which is traditionally called "contradictory" nor what is called "contrary." It is basically nothing but the disjunction of incompatibles. This becomes clear when we consider that possibly the same relation can hold between the objects A and C, and B and C, even if A and B are incompatible and insofar "contraries." For example, green is not only incompatible with red but also with purple which, in turn, also is incompatible with red. But the opposite in which we are interested is one whose members are of a special duality in such a manner that when two objects are opposite in this way then none of these objects can be opposite to a third object in the same way. Our relation of opposites has this characteristic in common with that relation of opposites which, in modern psychology itself, is called "contrast" and which has been largely ignored by traditional formal logic. The (psychological) contrast is the relationship which holds between the last members of an ordered series. In spite of the apparent kinship, our relation of opposites is not a psychological contrast. It is obvious that it holds between members which are capable of gradation. It does not hold, as does contrast, between certain (extreme) determinations of degrees, but it holds already between incomplete objects whose determinations are those degrees. Thus, similarity and difference can be determined by degrees. And there is a contrast between great and minimal similarity and difference, and, by virtue of the law of coincidence there is a contrast between equality and sufficiently great difference. Our relation of opposites, however, already holds between similarity and difference without consideration of such determinations. It even holds, in many respects more clearly, between being and not-being of the positiveness of the objective[2] which is called "negative." It is not comparable with not-being and non-smoker which amounts to the attempt to make our opposite a contradiction. The relationship between being and not-being / (p. 47) is the same as value and

---

[1]   Ad incomplete objects comp. **Über Möglichkeit und Wahrscheinlichkeit**, index.

[2]   Comp. **Ann. II**, p. 328 f.

negative value (*Unwert*) and must (*Sollen*) and must-not (*Nichtsollen*) (taken as the analogy of negative value). These considerable parallels[3] are affirmation and negation, pleasure and displeasure, desire and repulsion, that is, the experiences which present those objects[4]. The situation is not different with objects like warm and cold, sweet and bitter[5], right and left, up and down, high and low (of space or sound or whatever), big and small, much and little, and others, although, in respect to the latter examples, there is a tendency to think of extreme opposites. Surely there are many such opposites. But if I am correct, then incompletely determined objects are already opposite, which is exactly what we are speaking about here. This relation seems to need a special name, and we will call it the relation of polar opposites. And the members of this relation are polar opposites.

I do not know, at present, how to add to the characterization of "polar opposites" because it seems to be already quite clear. As has been said, the relation of polar opposites holds between incomplete objects and not just between objects which have been completely determined. The totality of the complete differentiating[6] determinates of each of the two members of (polar) opposites amounts to a quantitative series whose limits approach zero in which the correlated series, in a manner of speaking, converge. Accordingly, the linear illustrations of the two series can be joined at their zero points. Then the series run in opposite directions so that the two polar opposite objects are continuously linked by their gradations, and both together can be represented by a straight line. The continuous link via zero is especially remarkable because some other continuous link which is not quantitative / (p. 48) but qualitative seems to be impossible. The determinates which occupy a half line are naturally mutually incompatible. However, it is possible that they are so infinitesimally incompatible with the points on the other half line

---

3   Comp. St. Witasek "Über die ästhetische Objektivität," **Zeitschrift für Philosophie und philosophische Kritik**, Vol. CLVII, p. 105 (reprint, p. 19).

4   Comp. **Üb. Emot. Präs. (Em. Pres.)**, especially p. 44 ff.

5   There are also the opposites "sweet" and "sour" which contradict the condition of the duality of the opposite members which was given above. Or perhaps both of these pairs do not belong here.

6   Ad "differentiations" (*differentiative*) in contrast to "additive" determinations, comp. **Möglichk.**, p. 329 et al.

that they may even coincide quite lawfully, as is the case in the double series of potiores, which is also supported by the fact that the quantitative series are series of potiores and that coinciding points are complements. The question is if perhaps all polar objects form double series of potiores. At first, it does not seem that there is an affirmative answer to the question: for example, different degrees of value do not coincide with different degrees of negative value. But it is amazing how one feels involuntarily motivated to expect such a coincidence. Thus, the opposites heavy and light have, for a long time, been taken to be natural opposites based on the relatively extreme position in the quantitative series of objects of sensation[7], where "heavy" meant "very heavy" and "light" meant "barely heavy." But experimental psychology replaced such relativistic notions with "absolute impressions" which can be quantitatively graded. One can easily imagine that the degrees of "heaviness" (in the narrow sense) and of "lightness" are pictured on a straight line whose zero point or point of indifference is on its middle. If there is any sense in judging that "light" is also "barely heavy" and that "heavy" is also "barely light," it can be understood in a relativistic sense. But the thought of coincidence and complementarism cannot be discarded in the light of the fact of "absolute impression." In addition, it is known that several theoretical attempts have been made to take qualitative series, as e.g. the series of sound pitches to be binary compounds of opposite and quantitatively variable components. There is no justification today in making the sweeping statement that polar objects, in general, are capable of forming quantitative series or even double series of potiores. But such series seem to occur only in connection with polar objects, and it is possible that it can be shown, one day, / (p. 49) by a suitable approach, that there are such double series even in connection with those polar objects where they seem to be missing.

It is quite obvious that the analogy of the Law of Omission, as was shown in the relation of the terms I - IV, applies to polar objects which form double series of potiores. If I is not, then in any case II is or III or IV. If II is, then III is in any case according to the law of coincidence.

---

[7] "Objects of sensation" (*Empfindungsgegenstände*) must be understood in the sense of St. Witasek's **Grundlinien der Psychologie**, 1908 Reg. p. 213.

But if IV is, then the being of III follows a potiori. If I is not, then III must be, at any rate. If II is not, then I cannot be either because it is the potius of II. Likewise III is not because it coincides with II. Consequently, only IV remains. It is obvious that from the not-being of IV and III, the being of II and I can be inferred by analogy.

What is the situation in cases which are analogous to the Law of Omissions and where we cannot, without difficulties, fall back on the double series of potiores? Considering the examples given so far, we can say that in each case they concern mutually polar objects. "Much and little" is a pair of polar objects which concern available goods or the willingness to part with such goods. The same holds for "revenue and waste" (*Einnahme und Ausgabe*) and "must-be and must-not-be" (*sein sollen und nicht sein sollen*). After what has just been said, it does not appear audacious anymore to expect double series of potiores in connection with the first two of the just-recalled examples. The law which was derived in general terms above applies to them also. In respect to the other two examples, we must content ourselves with deliberations which are adapted to the special nature of the situation. In each case we find the function of contradictory opposites as they were introduced by definition. "May-do" *(Dürfen)* by definition is nothing else than the negation of the "must-do" *(Sollen)* of the opposite quality of being. Likewise, "expenditure" *(Entgang)* and "savings" *(Ersparnis)* are the negations of "revenue" *(Einnahme)* and "waste" *(Ausgabe)* respectively. The validity of our law is based on the form "If it is not the case that A is B, then it is the case that A is not B." This statement is not correct of undetermined objects[8], but it is immediately evident for complete objects.

---

8   Comp. **Über Möglichkeit und Wahrscheinlichkeit**, pp. 146, 594.

Section 3, Part III
The Law of Omission

/ (p. 50) *Chapter Fifteen*

The Law of Omission in Comparison
with Analogous Cases

In the foregoing, we have not considered all analogies of the Law of Omission. Even with the limited number of examples we have not been able to reach uniform results. But whatever we have found so far may yield sufficient basic information from which we can directly turn to the Law of Omission, and the question is if the Law of Omission has a still deeper kinship with cases which are already analogous to it. In fact, the Law of Omission manifests itself in two mutually polar objects. There we are dealing with value and negative value, or rather, degrees of value and of negative value, which can be illustrated – as was already mentioned – in two straight lines which meet at their zero points and run in opposite directions. Beside this, however, the comparison reveals essential differences, and the most important ones will be discussed in this study.

It need not be mentioned that I and IV - the numerals being used as before - are not points but line segments. For even the must and the too-much of our examples are not points. However, an important condition for the Law of Omission is the characteristic of occupying a line segment. This does not seem to be fulfilled in the examples of analogous cases. The correlation of I and III, II and IV is very tight here, since each degree of the points of one line corresponds to a definite point on the other line. The absence of an act of willing which is of a certain degree of merit is correlated with a certain degree of admissibility. The absence of an act of willing of a certain degree of correctness is correlated with a certain degree of reprehensibility. On the other hand, from the not-being *(Nichtbestand)* of the factuality of a being, the possibility of a not-being can be inferred, however, without further determination of degree, because different cases can involve very different possibilities of not-being. For if we make the conclusion "if it is not the case that some S is P then no S is P." / (p. 51) Then, any gradual differentiation in respect to II and IV is naturally excluded. It is clear that in this respect the analogy of the Law of Omission does not hold too well where, instead of I and IV, II and III are points, as, for example, must do *(Sollen)* and may do *(Dürfen)*. Whatever lies between too much and too little is certainly, like savings *(Ersparniss)* and expenditure *(Entgang)*, capable of degrees and occupies therefore a line segment: but it enters our lawful order as negation which as such is not capable of gradation and cannot be correlated by degrees with anything else in the sense of our law. There is another, even more obvious, difference in the double series of potiores as far as for them those coincidences are essential which are subordinate to the law of complements. These coincidences concern foremost the domains of I and III, and also play an important part in the derivation of the principal law *(Hauptgesetz)*. The Law of Omission also concerns the series of potiores. However, complements and associated coincidences are not of interest now. Thus, gradual determinations within the four sections of the value line and even different points of the value line are generally mutually incompatible with each other. This holds especially for the correct and admissible, that is, II and III. Occasionally[1] the desideratum is expressed in connection with them, that they should come close to a double series of potiores, but it cannot be fulfilled. However, we found that the analogy of the Law of

---

[1] Alois Höfler "Abhängigkeitsbeziehungen zwischen Abhängigkeitsbeziehungen," p. 51.

Omission occurs also independently of the coincidences of the double series. But also there are incompatibilities of the kind similar to the various points on the value line.

If coordination and compatibility are properties which character-ize, clearly although indirectly, the difference in the situation at hand, then there is another difference which is immediately obvious and fundamental once we determine with which the Law of Omission and with which the laws which are its analogies are concerned. Let us con-sider the recently mentioned inference from the absence of a factual objective to the possibility of its opposite objective. Then the result is as follows: it is not the case that a certain objective a is factual, from this it follows that the objective / (p. 52) non-a, as we will call it more briefly then clearly, is possible to some degree. Factuality and possibility seem to be attributes of objectives: consequently, whatever seems to be lawfully linked are objectives of being thus-and-so[2]. The same can be said of all other analogies of the Law of Omission. But what is our Law of Omis-sion itself about? It is about commission (*Setzung*) and omission. Commission and omission are not likely to be objectives of being thus-and-so. In fact, this law says that if an act of willing is absent and if, under certain conditions, it would be admissible or reprehensible or meritorious or correct, then the outcome is permissible or reprehensible or meritorious or correct respectively. Thus, if the meritorious is not, then the permissible is. If the correct is not, then the reprehensible is, and so forth. Objectives of being are lawfully correlated here; not so objectives of being thus-and-so. For a long time the difference between these two kinds of objectives had been totally ignored or had been discarded by the attempt to reduce existential judgments (or better, judgments of being) to categorical judgments or to reduce categorical judgments to existential judgments[3]. But in reality the thus-reduced judgments retained their particular character which merely became more or less latent. Only a transition from an objective of lower order to an objective of higher order was made. So far, the contrast between being

---

[2] This must not be confounded with the objectives a and non-a of our schematic example which could be objectives of being as well as objectives of being thus-and-so.

[3] Comp. especially F. Brentano, **Psychologie,** 1974, Vol. I, pp. 279 ff and 283 and, on the other hand, my discussions in **Gött. Gel. Anz.,** 1890.

and being thus-and-so must be recognized to be irreducible and fundamental. In fact, the Law of Omission should admit of the following
conclusion if at all it is likened to the other cases: "it is not the case that a
certain act of willing is meritorious; therefore, it must be permissible."
It is immediately clear that this is not at all true.

Having compared the Law of Omission with various seeming
analogies from fields outside of ethics, we get an utterly negative result:
the analogous cases are of no help in the understanding of our law when
the just shown differences are taken into consideration. Still, we cannot
dispense with the theoretical / (p. 53) attempt to reach an understanding.
A clarification of the discrepancy of this law with the nature of counter
feelings and counter values as shown above[4] is urgently needed. But
whosoever attempts to tackle this problem must take note of the following: the Law of Omission deals with the meritorious, correct, permissible, and reprehensible. Without a doubt, these are value classes. But the
foregoing characterizations are not really differentiations of values but
of obligations *(Sollen)*, as is quite clear. Thus, any attempt to penetrate
deeper into the Law of Omission must include expressly the problem of
obligation *(Sollen)* if it is expected to be successful at all. Consequently,
it will be put off to a time when we will take a closer look at the concept of
obligation in ethics. [17]

---

4 Comp. Ms. (p. 32).

Section 3, Part IV
Laws of Moral Values

Chapter Sixteen

Preliminary Remarks

Now, we direct our attention to the magnitude of the moral value as far as it is determined for the ego and for the alter by the magnitude of the values which play a part in the ego's and alter's respective decisions. On the way, investigations concerning this subject matter made years ago[1] will be corrected and completed. At first, symbols which will be used will be introduced and their meanings will be explained. The intentions of the use of these symbols will be explained as they occur in our more or less formalized discussions.

The symbols γ, g, υ, u relate to the first chapter of this book[2]; they are easily explained. Latin letters denote values for the self *(Selbstwerte)*; Greek letters denote values for the other *(Fremdwerte)*. If the occasion arises that symbols are needed to designate neutrality values, / (p. 54) we will use cursive letters *(g, u)*. In symbols of the same script there are different value prefixes. For Example, for υ we write -γ, for u we write -g. It remains to be determined if the represented values are egoistic, altruistic, or neutral. But if needed they can be designated by

---

[1] Comp. **Psych. eth. Unters.,** [p. 112]*.
[2] Comp. Ms. [p. 1 ff]*.

indices[3], moreover, by e, a, and n in the script of the main symbol to which the index is attached. Only Greek and Latin letters are main symbols, neutrality values are, as we have seen, neither egoistic nor altruistic[4]. Thus, only the index n can be attached to them, which may as well be left out because it does not indicate any differentiation.

For the time being, and as far as our immediate demands are concerned, we can do very well without Latin or Greek indices. But we must restrict ourselves, at first, to considering only values in themselves *(Eigenwerte)* and values for the other *(Fremdwerte)*. These values will be labeled with our main symbols and without indices. This arrangement naturally limits our area of investigation considerably. But, for the time being, it is worth simplifying our problem in this way, and we are justified in doing so. For the same purpose I will go one step further and will not even consider all egoistic values but will neglect quality values *(Eigenschaftswerte)* and consider only values of experience *(Erlebniswerte)* of the egoistic domain. Thus, for the time being, g and u shall designate experience goods *(Erlebnisgüter)* and experience misfortunes *(Erlebnisübel)* of the ego, γ and υ only experience goods or experience misfortunes of the alter. But the reservation must be made that the just introduced limitations of values will be given up as soon as the progress of our investigations will permit or even necessitate.

---

[3] Comp. **Psych. eth. Unters**, [p. 112]*.
[4] Comp. Ms. (p. 15).

Section 3, Part IV
Laws of Moral Values

Chapter Seventeen

The First Main Formula (*Hauptformel*)

In order to determine the object of moral value, I will take it for granted, in accordance with pre-scientific convictions, that, for this purpose, not the action but the act of willing is relevant. / (p. 55) The possibility is not excluded that actions may also enter the focus of our interest[1]. The use of the word "moral" may better agree with the convention[2] as differentiated from the use of the word "ethical" if the meaning of the word "moral" is not expanded beyond usual convention. Moreover, I have shown[3] as clearly as possible that for the determination of the moral value object it is not sufficient to consider the intention. For even in the simplest cases which are surely clear enough we must refer to certain concomitant value facts in order to get to the impersonal concern (*Anteil*)[4] which plays the controlling part. I have tried to make clear with a few simple formal notations in which way moral value

---

[1] Comp. for example, B. H. Pichler, **Grundzüge einer Ethik**, Graz, 1919, Introduction.

[2] Comp. Ms. (p. 27).

[3] **Psych. eth. Unters.**, pp. 94 f, 110.

[4] Ibid., pp. 158, 203.

depends upon intention and concomitant value objects; and I did not underestimate the obstacles resulting from such a plan, namely, that at present a quantitative determination of values cannot be achieved[5]. I designated the two main formulas and inferences which can be obtained from them as short expressions of the laws which I had discovered. Today I still believe that they are an adequate representation considering that they are concise expressions.

Nevertheless, a certain danger remains that, if this consideration is overlooked, then, by using simple numerals to signify constants, a semblance of precision may be evoked which is utterly unobtainable under the given circumstances. Moreover, I must admit that the lawfulness expressed in the formulae are not as obviously empirical as it seemed to me when I put them on paper[6]. This is automatically clear, especially in connection with borderline transitions; and it does not diminish the relevance of the lawfulness in question when, in this way, the apriori character becomes apparent. Perhaps it helps to clarify the whole situation if we investigate the cases exhibiting a lawfulness, not by investigating the acts of willing directly, / (p. 56) but by investigating the concerns on which the acts of willing are based. Perhaps we will even succeed in penetrating a little deeper into certain antagonistic tendencies which made the interpretation of the second and, then, also the first main formula difficult[7].

Concern [A]* is not an experience but a disposition for experiences, that is, for those experiences for which such secondary valuations are characteristic of which we found[8] that they are at the core of altruistic feelings and desires. If the ego values something because it is of (objective or only subjective) value for the alter, he activates his concern. This concern will be greater for the ego the more he values the object of the value for the alter (*Fremdwerte),* and the smaller the value is for the alter as value subject for whose sake the objectum in question is a value of a given magnitude for the ego. In shorter terms: the concern is the greater, *ceteris paribus,* the greater the secondary value is and the

---

5 **Psych. eth. Unters.,** Par. 46.
6 **Psych. eth. Unters.,** par. 46, pp. 131 ff.
7 Comp. ibid., [par. 50 and 51].
8 Comp. ibid., pp. 113 f.

smaller the primary value is which accompanies it. Let us call the concern "A," the objectum of the feeling of secondary value g to which the index "a" is attached. The index is against our symbolic conventions but it serves a useful purpose, as will be seen shortly. As a first try let the following formula stand:

$$A = \frac{g_a}{\gamma}$$

We did not especially consider prefixes, but the consideration occurs automatically. Primary and secondary valuations can have positive and negative prefixes. Thus, two cases of the same direction (pleasure in someone else's pleasure, sorrow in some else's sorrow; that is, being happy for someone and feeling compassion for someone *(Mitfreude und Mitleid)*, stand opposite two cases of opposite direction (pleasure in someone else's sorrow and sorrow in someone else's pleasure), that is, enjoyment of another's sorrow and jealousy *(Schadenfreude und Neid)*. When we take misfortune as a negative good then in cases of attitudes of the same direction, the result will be positive concern; in cases of attitudes of different directions, the result will be negative concern, which is quite natural. In a graph, put the positive and negative values of γ on the abscissa and the positive and negative values of g_a on the ordinate; / (p. 57) then each straight line running through the origin of the co-ordinates represents a concern of a certain magnitude. Each straight line which crosses the abscissa at a right angle represents, with increasing distance from the abscissa, increasing degrees of concern; each straight line crossing the ordinate at a right angle represents, with increasing distance from the ordinate, decreasing degrees of concern.

This way of representing concerns still leaves open what their constancy or variability may be under different circumstances. But it may be surmised that the concern of a subject at a given time is represented by a γ and a co-ordinate g_a in such a way that all g_a values belonging to the γ values lie on a straight line which continues through the origin of the co-ordinates. But then experience shows a different situation. This is apparent in the obvious case where γ and the co-ordinate g_a have the same, that is, positive prefixes. At first, it seems to be obvious that when I am interested in a small advantage of the alter, then I should be interested in a greater advantage of the alter. But if the γ is very large, it may easily happen that one envies one's neighbor for his luck. Then, the g_a does not have a positive but a negative prefix and increases again with the increase of the g. An analogous but rarer situation with different prefixes makes matters clearer. There, the ego values positively the alter's sorrow and not negatively, as might be expected. When the -γ is relatively small, this seems to happen quite frequently, and it seems to be consistent with expectations that in such cases when there is little interest in a small υ that there should be a greater interest in a greater υ, and the greater it is the better. However, experience shows that human nature is better than that: when υ grows, sympathy awakens and becomes more prominent with the growing magnitude of the υ.

In the two remaining cases where the ego reacts to γ and υ with a negative valuation, the attitude of the ego can be observed to go through a similar change of prefixes with increasing γ and υ. Anyone feeling sympathy for the alter's small sorrow feels deeper sympathy with his greater sorrow. Whoever gets upset over someone's small fortune gets even more upset over his greater fortune.

It is clear that the small amount of information / (p. 58) which we obtained from experience about these matters is really not sufficient for the construction of curves. But in order to illustrate the small amount of information which we do have, the following schematic may be useful. [18]

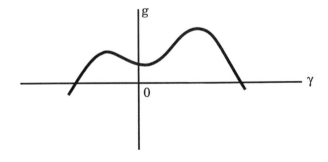

The curve to the right of the ordinate axis represents the course of sympathetic pleasure (*Mitfreude*), the curve to the left of the ordinate axis represents malicious pleasure (about someone's misfortune). The prefix changes of the values of the ordinate become apparent when the curve crosses the abscissa.

The curve of sympathetic pleasure crosses the abscissa at a greater distance from the zero point than the curve of malicious pleasure. This expresses the experience that all in all envy sets in later than sympathy. It is not quite certain, but experience gives sufficient support for setting the maximum of sympathetic pleasure higher than that of malicious pleasure. But these attempts at pinpointing lawful regularities are in need of diligent and, in particular, experimental examination. Moreover, the whole drawing is arbitrary and was executed with the desire to make the situations visually clear.

Visual representation suggests that the change of prefixes results from superpositioning two curves, one of which originally contains positive values whereas the other originally contains negative values. This would mean that each γ of the alter should be capable of evoking pleasure or sorrow in the ego. The result of the combination of the two feelings surfaces in the value attitude of the ego. But that the same objectum attracts simultaneously pleasure and sorrow contradicts all that seems to be rational / (p. 59) or even evident[9] as far as counter feelings are concerned. There are no difficulties when the opposite value feelings, strictly speaking, do not refer to the same objectum. That may well be the case where sympathy and envy seem to coincide. Direct experience shows clearly that there is a relativistic momentum in envy. Whatever evokes envy is not the absolute magnitude of the γ but its relation to values which belong to the ego or seem to belong to the ego. The unhappy person envies the happy person whose happiness he would not envy if his own fortune would not lag so far behind his own desires. It is clear that under these circumstances small γ's evoke envy to a much lesser degree than large γ's. If this interpretation is correct we must expect great variations in the distances of the points (from the ordinate) in which the resulting curve crosses the abscissa.

---

[9] Comp. **Zur Grundlegung der allgemeinen Werttheorie**, 1923, par. 2, [p.83 f]*.

We can apply analogous considerations to attitudes toward υ, i.e., someone else's sorrow. Without a doubt, sympathy is the natural reaction by the u of the ego to the υ of the alter, and the υ is simply taken at its absolute value. On the other hand, since ancient times the "*socios habuisse malorum*" has been taken to be gratifying. And there are always "innocent" jokes and teasing remarks in which the victim fares rather badly but not too badly. These are comparative cases, and there are many others, which give testimony to the fact that the ego feels superior to the alter in his satisfaction in his own good fortune, as long as the alter's situation is not too far removed from his own. "Malicious pleasure" *(Schadenfreude)* is perhaps too strong an expression for that attitude. At any rate, we are dealing here again with a relativistic momentum which, sooner or later, is usually overcome by an absolute momentum.

So far, we have only discussed cases with the same prefix in connection with which valuations with the opposite prefix occurred so-to-speak on the sidelines and which permitted a relativistic interpretation. Without a doubt, there are cases of (a person's) concern with opposite prefixes where a relativistic consideration does not apply. The pleasure of the alter may bring with it, from the very beginning, the sorrow of the ego, / (p. 60) the sorrow of the alter may bring with it the pleasure of the ego. There it is ill will or envy; here it is malicious pleasure or even cruelty in the proper sense of the word. The resulting negative concern grows with the decreasing value for the other *(Fremdwerte)*, as it is given to the ego, and with the decreasing value for the self *(Selbstwert)* which consequently results for the ego. Complications resulting from superpositioning of curves do not seem to occur.

If the foregoing is correct, we can summarize as follows: secondary valuations of the ego which refer to primary valuations of the alter clearly express how the ego is concerned with the well-being or woe of the alter. [19]

Section 3

/ (p. 61) Meinong's Additional Notes to The Fragment: *Elements of Ethics*

[1] ad (p. 1).

Concerning ethical individualism, compare E. Honneffer "Der moderne Individualismus," **Kantstudien** XXXIII, #4, 1919, especially pp. 412 ff, 423 ff - Humboldt's humanitarian ideal (**Geschichte der Philosophie**, Überweg IV, 11th ed., p. 63 ff).

If we make a difference between dispositional value and actuality value *(Aktualiätswert),* then we may have to differentiate also between that which is willed and the action without considering the intentions involved. Comp. Pichler **Grundzüge einer Ethik**, Graz, 1919, p. 5.

Mere consideration of mental attitudes as being one-sided, ibid. bottom of page. Consideration of intentions and motives *(Beweggründe)* is merely a matter of differentiation, ibid. p. 6, comp. p. 10.

Other-feelings *(Fremdgefühle)*, Groethuisen, **Zeitschrift für Psychologie,** Vol. 34, pp. 242 f.

Against the term "altruistic," ibid. p. 244, Footnote 1, comp. text, altruistic according to Spencer ibid. p. 259 top.

Axioms concerning motivation and egoism, Schopenhauer, **Grundlagen der Moral**, pp. 288 f, Reclam edition.

[2] ad (p. 4).

It seems that neutrality values can be considered to be exclusively impersonal values. But then one should say at once "impersonal value" instead of "neutrality value" in order to avoid mistaking it for "neutral value."

[3] ad (p. 4).

Self-enlargement *(Selbsterweiterung)* as opposed to altruism (Pichler, **Ethik**, p. 36).

The object is supposedly essential for egoism. Lipps, **Ethische Grundfragen**, 2nd ed., p. 10, especially pp. 37 ff. But is the desire for a keepsake egoistic? Is the desire to acquire a certain skill not egoistic?

Difference between one's own and someone else's experience concerns merely personal proximity. Lipps, **Ethische Grundfragen**, 2nd ed., pp. 130f, comp. p. 144.

Ipsism, Thieme (Külpe introduction, 8th ed., p. 379 footnote)

[4] ad (p. 6).

(ad missing and supplemented manuscript, leaf 10) It must be expressly denied that not all valuations are egoistic, comp. **Psych.-eth. Unt. zur. Wertth.**, pp. 96 ff.

[5] ad p. 8.

The thesis which was discussed on leaf 10 (supplement (p. 6)) does not differ clearly from the first statement about egoism which was refuted above. / (p. 62) The point of view taken there also contradicts the position that all desires can be traced to valuations.

[6] Ad (p. 11).

H. Pichler, **Ethik,** pp. 35 ff describes self-enlargement as resulting from self-denial *(Entselbstung)* and self-assertion *(Selbstbehauptung)*. It can be objected that self-enlargement, even in the sense of p. 36

((p. 36) above) is merely a value transfer from an immediate to a more remote subject, that is, it is supposedly presupposed in self-denial (*Entselbstung*).

[7] ad (p. 16).

Is the characterization of the neutral as given here really positive? The exclusion of "mine" is essential.

[8] ad (p. 17).

More detail concerning the characterization of altruistic behavior. Comp. Lipps, **Ethische Grundfragen,** pp. 31 ff.

It is of lower priority in comparison with egoistic attitudes. According to Lipps the reason is that the reproductions of feelings are important for altruism, but that feelings and other experiences themselves are important for egoism. But this is not correct because a feeling of sympathy is as much an actual experience (*Ernsterlebnis*) as those on which egoistic attitudes are based.

On the other hand, it is also correct if one does not consider the secondary value feeling as much as that experience by which the ego apprehends the value position of the alter. I apprehend the physical pain of another person through a fantasy feeling. Therefore my sympathy with the pain of the other person is usually not quite adequate.

But where does altruistic value feeling give the impetus for a fantasy feeling when in fact a certain property of the objectum is characteristic for the secondary feeling, the property namely to be, at the same time, a value objectum for the alter? It lies apparently in a characteristic determination which I can apprehend with the help of a fantasy value feeling. There, the strength of my actual secondary feeling depends largely upon the degree (high or low) with which I can accomplish this fantasy feeling, or it depends on my ability, that is, my attribute, to put myself into the place of the other person - as one says rather misleadingly. To put myself into the place of the other person does not consist in assuming that I am the other person but in assuming that I am in the situation of the other person; and this is a great help for my apprehending fantasy. It is often said of physicians that they prescribe a diet for the patient which they like best for themselves. One does not have sympathy with a situation which one cannot fantasize concretely (*anschaulich*) or which one in fact does not fantasize concretely.

Nature of Altruism. Altruism and Love

It is often said that altruism is love of one's fellow man. Benevolence toward a loved person is taken for granted. But if altruism is characterized by a value experience, then that seems to mean that also love is only a value experience. But it is apparent that a valuation is too cold for that. Lipps, **Eth. Grundfragen**, p. 28, indicates that perhaps we should love inanimate objects which are useful to us. If that is the case, where is the difference?

It does not matter much, here, to assume that love is a disposition. It is not only a disposition for a single feeling, a value feeling, but also for an affect, an emotion (*Gemütsbewegung*) which is much more complicated. In this complex, the valuation, which after all is altruistic, plays an important role. There we could find / (p. 63) a characteristic part of love which Lipps describes inadequately as empathy (*Einfühlung*), the capability and inclination to put oneself into (the place of) the other person. Perhaps it is characteristic that the ego likes the alter because of his character or because of some of his actions, that is, the alter is valuable to the ego whereby the characteristic secondary valuations of altruism need not be considered. Most of this and the best remains psychologically unexplained.

[9] ad (p. 17 f.).

Concerning further development of the concept of egoism:

When egoism is determined by the very close association of value objectum and ego, a pointed interpretation is added: neglect or damage of the alter's interests. It is not yet egoistic when I pursue my own interests, but when I pursue them exclusively, that is, in conflict with the interests of others, then it is egoistic.

It can be asked under which circumstances that special relationship to the ego which is essential to egoism is established. The most
natural path to a result is a) the objectum of value, valuations, or desire
must be an inner or external experience, b) the motive of the valuation
must be an inner experience.

Furthermore, ad a) one's own psychic states as objecta, comp.
Psych.-eth. Unters..., especially Ehrenfels' **Werttheorie I**, pp. 107 ff.
Foremost case: pleasure but also ideas, thought experiences. Examples
of sensations: sensations of temperature and taste, but also physical
states as health and illness.

ad b) pleasure *(Lust)* (which itself may not be a valuation) does
not have to be an object, it can also act as motive - as when I value taste or
temperature because they are pleasant. Besides emotional motives there
are also intellectual motives; all presuppositions, at least secondary presuppositions *(Voraussetzungen)*, can be considered as motives. But I can
share intellectual motives with other subjects. If I value an invention
because it is especially original, then everyone else who recognizes its
originality can value it: the intellectual motive is no guaranty that the
objectum stands in that exclusive relationship which is the condition for
egoism. If it is not feasible to limit intellectual motives to a single subject (and that will be difficult to accomplish), then only an emotional
motive can serve as an isolating motive.

Values of that kind can be called experience values. The value
of the experience itself, of life, of self-preservation, and anything related
to it, can be counted as quasi-experience value.

Whatever is derived from experience values when they are
parent values or original values imposes a limitation. Value feelings
which originate by association can be included. All of these values can
be subsumed under the label of experience value in a wider sense of the
word.

My own relatively lasting attributes (primarily dispositions,
perhaps also other things?) are exclusively limited to myself just as my
experiences are. Therefore egoistic values of experience can be co-
ordinated with quality values *(Erlebniswerte, Eigenschaftswerte)*, and
the properties are physical as well as psychological. Anything which is

egoistic refers either to values of experience or property values and to nothing else.

/ (p. 64) Altruistic values of experience and property values must be differentiated in the same manner as egoistic values. Derived and transferred values have to be appropriately counted among them. Also here is the quasi-value of experience: life (of course, of the alter) in a quasi position for the reason that its valuation does not, without reservation, depend upon the alter's valuation of it. Still, the fact of altruism remains present because of the presumption that the life of the alter has value absolutely, even if the alter does not value it. Such a presumption, in an appropriate attitude toward the alter, as it seems to be at the basis of all love, is not empirically noticeable.

Egoistic values can be derived from egoistic values of experience by transfer or even by association. For altruistic values this is true for derivation by transfer, it is not true of all derivations by association but only those which take place in the alter. The latter derivations may also take place in the ego because secondary value is a value at which association can begin. For example, the good memories which I have of a friend proceed from an altruistic valuation of his character and life. But the memory itself is not altruistic. That can be obscured by the fact that it originates from an altruistic valuation. Normally the value of the remembrance will be egoistic which is not the fault of the remembrance whose value may also be neutral even if someone else, instead of me, is the subject of the value. Goethe's garden house in Jena (must be Weimar, trans.), Schubert's birth place are memorials of neutral value.

[10] ad (p. 21).

Apparently the paragraph intends to show that there can be a relationship of value transfer between disposition and action (*Leistung*). But the capability of values to be transferred from action to disposition was the starting point of the whole discussion of the values of dispositions. It cannot be introduced here as something new. However, it is indeed peculiar that a disposition which in itself is valuable can be repressed, under certain conditions, by special characteristics of the action.

The remark in the preceding paragraph that perhaps something is good because it is done by a good person belongs into the present context and must be put into this place.

[11] ad (p. 27).

Külpe, in his reference to phenomenology (**Einleitung in die Philosophie**, 8th ed., pp. 353 f) disregards the fact that we proceeded from the empirical description of the ethical in **Psychol. eth. Untersuchungen**.

[12] ad (p. 28).

Preference of the middle in knowledge (not too much, not too little). Compare H. Gomperz according to E. Zilsel, **Anwendungsproblem**, p. 100.

[13] ad (p. 30).

When the terms "ethical" and "moral" are introduced, it must be noted that these expressions, which in popular use are almost synonymous, have apparently been used by various authors for various conceptual differentiations, as e.g. by v. Ehrenfels in **System II** and also by Lipps in **Ethische Grundfragen** where, however, *Moralität* and *Sittlichkeit* are differentiated (beginning of book).

Omissions value and those of negative value as counter examples to intentional actions as condition for ethical value. Pichler, **Ethik**, p. 5. Lipps uses "correct" for (external) actions, **Ethische Grundfragen**, 2nd ed., p. 121.

/ (p. 65)

[14] ad (p. 31).

According to Pichler, **Ethik**, p. 9 correct and admissible can be determined only from the standpoint of omission, that is, from the standpoint of the reprehensible and the meritorious. But on the same page, a little further down, the claim seems to be revoked.

Exception of the law: when a commission is weakly approved, its omission is also weakly disapproved, ibid.

Primacy of disapproval over approval, ibid. Footnote 2.

H. Pichler, **Grundzüge einer Ethik**, Graz, 1919.

[15] ad (p. 37).

Concerning necessary possibility, there is a small correction in **Kausalgesetz** (A. Meinong, **Zum Erweise eines allgemeinen Kausalgesetzes,** 1918, p. 80) to which we refer at this place. Ibid. p. (?)

[16] ad (p. 41).

Permission, command, Gallinger (A. Gallinger, **Das Problem der objektiven Möglichkeit**, Leipzig 1912), **Objektive Möglichkeit,** pp. 52 f.

[At this place reference is made to parts of the work which remained unwritten.]*

[18] ad (p. 58).

The drawing is missing in the manuscript. [It was added to the manuscript by Prof Mally, the editors.]*

[19] ad (p. 60).

The manuscript ends abruptly. Only the following note appears:

Concerning Obligation (Sollen)

F. Weber [Prof. em. Franz Weber, Ljubljana, a student of Meinong]* law of obligation (**Sollensgesetz**) (still unpublished): the magnitude of obligation is zero if the possibility of the objective which ought to be is 1 and 0; if it is at its maximum when the possibility is 1/2.

Counter example: if the magnitude of obligation rises to 1/2, then there is no reason against its rising above that. But then we get contradictory results.

A counter argument: construct a double line of possibilities for the objective which ought to be, on the left factuality point, on the right infactuality point, being on the upper line, not-being on the lower line. Factuality-of-being implies the factuality of a lack of obligation or of must-not (*Nichtsollen*). This is reduced to 1/2 and beyond, so that it has the value zero at the point of infactuality. Such a line also corresponds to the point of infactuality and the possibilities of not-being. The former line of obligation, however, shall be drawn over the given double line, the latter line of obligation shall be drawn under the given double line. According to the law of complements, each of these lines of obligation corresponds to a complementary line so that two double lines of obliga- tion are given under and above the given double line. Thus, above and below the first drawn double lines two double lines of obligation are added. The upper line is above the line of ought-not (*Nichtsollen*), the lower line below the line of ought-not. The two lines of ought-not do not contradict each other. Moreover, the left half line on top and the right half line on the bottom represent the potius of the corresponding other half line. The half lines which are so-to-speak thus overcome do not conse- quently contain possibilities of ought-not. Therefore, the law of comple- ments, which is concerned with positive obligation, does not hold for them. Only those half lines remain for obligations which correspond to the main possibility of ought-not. The justified obligation occupies the whole line, depending on its magnitude, which, at its ends, has zero points and, in its middle, the value 1/2 - / (p. 66) just as it is supposed to be according to its law. The situation can be illustrated in this way: in the upper double line of obligation the right half of the line representing positive obligation is deleted, and in the lower line of obligation the left half of the line representing positive obligation is deleted.

Does the law admit of empirical verification? At first sight, duty is obligation and occurs in degrees. Are they accompanied by possibili- ties? The following may seem to be the case: duty may be the less binding the greater the desired (*beanspruchte*) g is. The greater the sacrifice is which is demanded of me, the smaller is the probability that I undertake it. Indeed, in the face of considerable improbability, my duty becomes small. In the face of great probability, my duty increases, whereas, according to the law, the maximum should lie in the middle, namely at 1/2.

On the other hand, there seems to be a different verification: it is not my duty to exert influence where I cannot have any influence; in the same way, it is not my duty to exert any influence where my influence is not required because the situation develops on its own accord. There, the maximum could really lie in the middle.

On the whole, the prospect of verification is not very favorable. The proper gradual changes of obligation go hand in hand with changes in the magnitudes of value. Are we dealing with variations of the law which are of utterly different dimensions?

Vocabulary

Ethische Bausteine,
Gesamtausgabe III
Elements of Ethics

German - English:

Anteil = concern (acc. to Findlay) p. 153/154

Ausgabe als Verschwendung? = waste ?

Betrag = value (not a technical term)

Eigengegenstand = proper object

Eigenschaftswert = quality values

Eigenwert = value in itself (A value which is independent of other values or of other objects, it has, as such, no connection with egoistic or altruistic interests.)

Einnahme = revenue (income?)

entferntes Subjekt = remote subject

Entgang = cost or loss, expenditure

Erlebnisgüter = experience goods

Erlebnisübel = experience misfortune

Erlebniswert = value of experience

Ersparniss = savings

Freigibigkeit = generosity

Fremdwert = value for the other

geboten = ordered, commanded

Geiz = miserliness

korrekt = correct (required, so Chisholm)

Meinheitsrelation = relation of mine

nächstes Subjekt = immediate subject

neutraler wert = neutral value

Neutralwert = neutrality value

Personwert = value for a person

Selbstwert = value for the self

Setzung = commission

Sparsamkeit = frugality

Stammwerte = parent values

Übertragungswert = transfer value

Überwert = Superior value, high positive value, supererogation!!

Unterlassungsgesetz = law of omission

Unterwert = negative value

Verschwendung = extravagance, prodigality

verwerlich = reprehensible

Wertabstufung = gradations of value

Wertbewegung = value movement

Wertstellung = value position

Wirkungswert = derived value

Zustandswert = situational value

English - German:

commanded, ordered = geboten

commission = Setzung

concern (acc. to Fidlay) = Anteil

correct (required acc. to Chisholm) = korrekt

derived value = Wirkungswert

experience goods = Erlebnisgüter

experience misfortune = Erlebnisübel

expenditure (also cost or loss) = Entgang

extravagance, prodigality = Verschwending

frugality = Sparsamkeit

generosity = Freigebigkeit

gradations of value = Wertabstufung

immediate subject = nächstes Subjekt

Law of Omission = Unterlassungsgesetz

miserliness = Geiz

negative Value = Unterwert

neutral value = neutraler Wert

neutrality value = Neutralwert

parent values = Stammwert

proper object = Eigengegenstand

quality value = Eiegnschaftswert

relation of mine = Meinheitsrelation

remote subject = entferntes Subject

reprehensible = verwerflich

revenue (income) = Einnahme

savings = Ersparniss

situational value = Zustandswert

superior value, high positive value (supererogation) = Überwert

transfer value = Übertragungswert

value (sometimes used as a non-technical term) = Betrag

value for a person = Personwert

value for the other = Fremdwert

value for the self = Selbstwert

value in itself = Eigenwert (A value which is independent of other values
or other objects, it has no connection with egoistic or altruistic values.)

value movement = Wertbewegung

value of experience = Erlebniswert

value position = Wertstellung

waste = Ausgabe

Bibliography

Primary Literature

Meinong, Alexius. **Gesamtausgabe**. Eds. R. M. Chisholm, R. Haller, R. Kindinger, and R. Fabian. Graz: Akademische Druck und Verlagsanstalt, 1969-1978

From Volume I: Hume Studien I (H.St.I)

From Volume II: Hume Studien II: Zur Relationstheorie Über Gegenstandstheorie (H.St.II)

From Volume III: Über emotionale Präsentation (Üb. em. Präs. or Em. Pres. in translation)

Psychologisch-ethische Untersuchungen zur Werttheorie (Psy.-Eth.Unt.)

Zur Grundlegung der allgemeinen Werttheorie (Grundlegung or Grdlegg.)

Ethische Bausteine, English: Elements of Ethics. (Eth. Baust. or Elem. Eth.)

From Volume IV: Über Annahmen, 2nd ed. (Ann.II)

From Volume V: Überdie Stellung der Gegenstandstheorie im System der Wissenschaften (Gegenstandstheorie or Gegstdsth.)

From Volume VI: Über Möglichkeit und Wahrscheinlichkeit (Mögl.)

From Volume VII: Selbstdarstellung, Vermischte Schriften (Verm. Schr.)

Ergänzungsband: Kolleghefte und Fragmente

Nachlass in the manuscript collection in the library of the University of Graz.

Secondary Literature

Austin, J. L. "Are there Apriori Concepts?" **Austin Philosophical Papers**, 2nd ed. Eds. J. O. Urmson and G. J. Warnock. Oxford: Oxford University Press, 1970

Ayer, A. J. "The Apriori," **Language, Truth, and Logic,** 2nd ed. London: Victor Gollancz, Ltd., 1946

Barber, K. "Meinong's Hume Studies, Part II: Meinong's Analysis of Relations," **Philosophy and Phenomenological Research**, Vol. XXXI, 1970

Bennett, Jonathan. **Kant's Analytic.** Cambridge: Cambridge University Press, 1966

---- "Analytic - Synthetic," **Proceedings of the Aristotel. Society**, Vol. 59, 1959

Meaning, Reference, and Necessity. Ed. Simon Blackburn. Cambridge: Cambridge University Press, 1975

Carnap, Rudolf. **Meaning and Necessity,** 2nd ed. Chicago: University of Chicago Press, 1956

Chisholm, Roderick M. "Contrary-to-Duty Imperatives and Deontic Logic." Analysis 24, 1963. pp. 33-36

---- "Supererogation and Offense, A Conceptual Scheme for Ethics," **Ratio**, Vol. V, 1963. pp. 1-14

---- **Theory of Knowledge**, 3rd. ed. Englewood Cliffs: Prentice Hall, 1977

--- "Brentano's Analysis of the Consciousness of Time," **MidWest Studies in Philosophy,** Vol. VI. 1981

---- **The Foundations of Knowing**. Minneapolis: University of Minnesota Press, 1982

Ewing, A. C. **The Fundamental Problems of Philosophy**. New York: Macmillan, 1951

Frege, Gottlob. **The Foundations of Arithmetic**, 2nd ed. New York: Harper and Rowe, 1953

Haack, Susan. **Philosophy of Logics**. Cambridge: Cambridge University Press, 1978

Jenseits von Sein und Nichtsein. Ed. Rudolph Haller. Graz: Akademische Druck und Verlagsanstalt, 1972

---- "Meinong's Gegenstandstheorie und Ontologie," **Journal of the History of Philosophy, IV**, 1966

---- "Incompleteness and Fictionality in Meinong's Objects Theory," **Topoi**, Vol. 8, 1989

Deontic Logic: Introductory and Systematic Readings. Ed. Risto Hilpinen. Dordrecht: D. Reidel Publishing Co., 1971

Hintikka, Jaakko. "Quantifiers in Deontic Logic" and "Deontic Logic and its Philosophical Morals," **Models for Modalities, Selected Essays** (by J. Hintikka). Dordrecht: D. Reidel Publishing Co., 1970. pp. 184-214

Kalsi, Marie-Luise Schubert. "Translation and Introduction," **Alexius Meinong: On Emotional Presentation.** Evanston, IL, Northwestern University Press, 1972

---- "On Evidence According to Meinong and Chisholm," **Philosophical Topics**, 1985

---- **Alexius Meinong on Objects of Higher Order und Husserl's Phenomenology**. Den Haag: Martinus Nijhoff Publishers, 1978

---- **Meinong's Theory of Knowledge**. Den Haag: Martinus Nijhoff Publishers, 1987

Kindinger, Rudolf. "Grundzüge der gegenstandstheoretischen Betrachtungsweise," **Unser Weg,** Vol. 13, 1958

Kitcher, Philip. "Apriori Knowledge," **The Philosophical Review**, Vol. 76, 1980

Kripke, Saul A. **Naming and Necessity.** Cambridge: Harvard University Press, 1980

Kroon, Frederick W. "Was Meinong Only Pretending?" **Phil. Phenomenol. Res., 52 (3),** 499-527. Spring '92 (Ontology, non-existing objects results of presentation)

Lambert, Karel. **Meinong and the Principle of Independence.** Boston: Cambridge University Press, 1983

---- "A Logical Reconstruction of Meinong's Theory of Independence," **Topoi.** 1983

---- "Unmögliche Gegenstände, eine Untersuchung der Meinong-Russell-Kontroverse," **Conceptus**, Vol. 11. 1977

Landmann-Kalischer, Edith. "Über den Erkenntniswert ästetischer Urteile," **Archiv für die Gesamte Psychologie**, Vol. V. 1905

"Essays in Honor of Roderick M. Chisholm," **Analysis and Metaphysics.** Ed. Keith Lehrer. Dordrecht/Boston: P. Reidel Publishing Co., 1975

Locke, Don. "The Necessity of Analytic Truth," **Philosophy**, Vol. 44. 1969

Luizzi, Vincent. **A Case for Legal Ethics**, State University of New York Press, 1993

Lycan William G. "Two - No, Three - Concepts of Possible Worlds," **Proc. Arist. Soc.**, Vol. 91, 1991. pp. 215-227

Mally, Ernst. "Über den Begriff des Gegenstandes in Meinong's Gegenstandstheorie," **Jahrbuch der Philosophischen Gesellchaft an der Universität zu Wien.** Leipzig: Ambrosius Barth, 1913

--- "Über die Unabhängigkeit der Gegenstände vom Denken," **Zeitschrift für Philosophie und philosophische Kritik**, Vol. 155. 1914

--- **Grundgesetze des Sollens: Elemente der Logik des Willens.** Graz: Leuschner und Lubensky, 1926

Marti-Huang, Duen Jau. **Die Gegenstandstheorie von Alexius Meinong als Ansatz zu einer ontologisch neutralen Logik.** Bern/Stuttgart: Verlag Haupt, 1984

Mates, Benson. "Analytic Sentences," **The Philosophical Review**, Vol. 60. 1951

Menger, Karl. "A Logic of the Doubtful. On Optative and Imperative Logic," **Reports of a Mathematical Colloquium, 2.** Notre Dame University, Indiana University Press, 1939. pp. 53-64

Apriori Knowledge, Oxford Readings in Philosophy. Ed. Paul K. Moser. Oxford: Oxford University Press, 1987

Austrian Philosophy, Studies and Texts. Ed. J. C. Nyiri. Munich: Philosophia Verlag, 1981

Pap, Arthur. "The Different Kinds of Apriori," **The Philosophical Review**, Vol. 53. 1944

Parsons, Terence. **Nonexistent Objects**. New Haven: Yale University Press, 1980

Platinga, Alvin. **The Nature of Necessity**. Oxford: Clarendon Press, 1974

Putnam, Hilary. **Mind, Language, and Reality, Philosophical Papers**. Cambridge: Cambridge University Press, 1975

---- "Analycity and Apriority: Beyond Wittgenstein and Quine," **Midwest Studies in Philosophy**, Vol. 4. Minneapolis: University of Minnesota Press, 1979

Ross , D. W. **The Right and the Good**. Oxford: Clarendon Press, 1930

Routley, Richard. "On the Durability of Impossible Objects," **Inquiry**, Vol. 19. 1976

--- "Rehabilitating Meinong's Theory of Objects," **Revue Internationale de Philosophie**, 104/5. 1973

--- **Exploring Meinong's Jungle and Beyond**. Research School of Social Science, Australian National University. 1979

Russell, Bertrand. **The Problems of Philosophy**. Oxford: Oxford University Press, 1912

Schlick, Moritz. **Allgemeine Erkenntnislehre**. Frankfurt/Main: Suhrkamp, 1979

Sellars, Wilfrid. "Is There a Synthetic Apriori?" **American Philosophers at Work**. Ed. Sidney Hook. New York: Criterion Books, 1956

Stenius, Eric. "Principles of a Logic of Normative Systems," **Proceedings of a Colloquium on Modal and Many-Valued Logics, (Acta Fennica** 16). Helsinki: 1963. pp. 247-260

---- **The Foundations of Ethics**. Oxford: Clarendon Press, 1939

Innate Idea. Ed. Stephen Stich. Berkeley: University of California Press, 1975

Twardowsky, Kasimir. **Inhalt und Gegenstand der Vorstellungen**, Einleitung Rudolf Haller. Munich: Philosophia Verlag, 1982

Wolf, Karl. "Dialektik des Gegenstandsbegriffes, von der Gegenstandstheorie Meinongs zur Wirklichkeitsphilosophie Mallys," **Wiener Zeitschrift für Philosophie, Psuchologie, Pädagogik,** Vol. II. 1948

--- "Die Grazer Schule; Gegenstandstheorie und Wertlehre," **Philosophie in Österreich.** 1968

von Wright, G. H. "Deontic Logic," **Mind** 60, (1951),1-15.

von Wright, G. H. **Studies.** London: Routledge and Kegan Paul, 1957

Zalta, Edward N. "On Mally's Alleged Heresy: A Reply," **History of Philosophical Logic,** Vol. 13 (1), 1992. pp. 59-68

Index

B

Bad, 49, 92
Beautiful, 44, 48, 49, 54
Beauty, 48, 54
Being thus-and-so, 8, 9, 47,
    152, 153
Benevolence, 53
Bolzano, 4
Brentano, 34
Brute fact, 28

C

Caesar, 34
Categorical judgments, 130
Causal relationship, 34, 63
Certainty, 12, 28, 52
Chisholm, 66, 68, 79
Class, 41
Classes, 39
Coincidences, 71
Commanded, 131
Commanded, allowed,
    forbidden, 142
Commanded, permitted, not-
    commanded, forbidden,
    139
Commission, 68, 125
Commission of acts, 67
Commission of volitions, 79
Complete, 35, 36, 41, 42, 43
Complete determination, 37
Complete objects, 33, 35, 41, 149
Completely abstract concepts,
    23

Completely apriori, 23
Completely determined, 19,
    37, 39, 42
Completely determined object,
    35
Completeness, 36, 38
Complexes, 4
Concept, 18, 20, 38, 42
Concept of egoism, 81
Concept, general, 21
Concept, non-contradictory,
    23
Concept, particular, 21
Conceptual determinations,
    22
Concrete, 19
Constant curves, 28
Content, 13, 20, 40
Contents, 28
Contingent, 143
Contradictories, 65
Contradictory, 146
Contradictory properties, 40,
    41, 42
Contraries, 65, 66, 75
Contrary, 146
Correct, 44, 66, 67, 68, 129, 151,
    153
Correct acts, 83
Correct desires, 45
Correct desiring, 54
Correct ideas, 54
Counter-feelings, 53, 80, 126
Counter-values, 8

D

E

N

O